Star Logic

(a collection of poiesis)

منطق النجم

(مجموعة من تكون)

من
سليمان ادريس

By
Solayman Idris

The Seal of Orun

بِسْمِ اللَّهِ الرَّحْمَنِ الرَّحِيمِ

In the Name of God
the Merciful
the Compassionate

Star Logic (a collection of poiesis)

ISBN: 978-1-7353273-5-8

Lumifont

Scriptorium

Published by Nafura Nawra Buruj Miraj
called Lumifont Scriptorium
Phone: 919.886.4447
Email: melanintelligence@gmail.com

Printed in the United States of America

وَمَا كَانَ النَّاسُ إِلَّا أُمَّةً وَاحِدَةً فَاخْتَلَفُوا وَلَوْلَا كَلِمَةٌ سَبَقَتْ مِن رَّبِّكَ لَقُضِيَ بَيْنَهُمْ فِيمَا فِيهِ يَخْتَلِفُونَ

And what was humanity;
except one nation?

So they disagree.

And has not the Word already
come down from your Lord;

To judge between them,
in what they disagree?

-Yunus, "Jonah", 10:19

I

But ye are a chosen
generation, a royal
priesthood, an holy nation,
a peculiar people;
that ye should shew forth the
praises of Him who hath
called you out of darkness
into His marvelous light:

Which in time past were not
a people, but are now the
people of God: which had not
obtained mercy, but now
have obtained mercy...

1 Peter 2 : 9 - 10

fiat justitia, ruat caelum:
****

(   ) (

*   *   *

let justice be done;
though the heavens fall
○○○

Sideris Sermo I

Sentient Dark : Fiat Lux

Table of Contents

Table of Contents

On Melanintelligence : Orun School Paperwork as Fugitive Intelligences

Orun is the only nation in human history to have dealt with transatlantic displacement, cultural erasure, and enforced illiteracy.[1] The psycho social wounds of continental African betrayal, middle passage trauma, and new world torture, are held in our hidden memories,[2] expressed in our combined anguish and triumph, and crystalized in our art and craft.[3] Our healing, treatment, medicants, justice, redemption, and legacies are hidden (t)here too. *And We sent knowledge into y'all from The First: Why don't y'all remember?*[4]

American founding fathers made active plans for Orun miseducation[5]: forbidding Orun to speak or write in our native Afro Arabic tongues and scripts; furthermore killing whites for teaching

---

[1] Women were forbidden education under the taliban in Afghanistan, Also currently in Xing Xang Province in China, there are untold abuses occurring.

[2] Alexander G. Halsberry and Sabine Gressler; *Epigenetics and Human Health: Linking Hereditary, Environmental and Nutritional Aspects:* Wiley - VCH, Verlag Gamb H & Co. KgaA, 2011

[3] Solayman Idris, *Star Logic (a Collection of Poiesis)* , Durham, NC, Lumifont Scriptorium 2020

[4] وَلَقَدۡ عَلِمۡتُمُ النَّشۡأَةَ الۡأُولَىٰ فَلَوۡلَا تَذَكَّرُونَ

"...And We sent knowledge into y'all from The Genesis: Why don't y'all remember?..."- Al Waqi'ah, "The Event" (56:62)

[5] Carter G. Woodson, *Miseducation of the Negro, Cambridge, Massachusetts,* Harvard University Press, *1933*

1

enslaved peoples to read in English.[6] Written and native communications were criminalized, in any language for Orun, on pain of death. Orun School, to a degree is ultimately derived from fugitive intelligences,[7] revealed for the true empowerment, of American Descendants of Slavery.[8]If they had their way, We would never have this Book.We would never write this Book....never read it.We would never share it.We would never be aware of it. *Be*[9] aware & share it.

---

[6] *Ronald A.T. Judy, Foreword by Wahneema Lubiano, DisForming the American Canon African-Arabic Slave Narratives and the Vernacular; Minneapolis, MN, University of Minnesota Press, 1993*

[7]*a.) "After the slave revolt led by Nat Turner in 1831, all slave states except Maryland, Kentucky, and Tennessee passed laws against teaching slaves to read and write."- Literacy as Freedom, The Smithsonian Institute and Art Museum, 2014*
***b.)** Janet Cornelius, We Slipped and Learned to Read:" Slave Accounts of the Literacy Process, 1830-1865; Phylon Vol. 44, No. 3 (1983) Publishedby: Clark Atlanta University.*
*c.) Melanintelligence = **darkness** ÷ fiat luX*
***d.)** "Renationalization", Star Logic, 2020*
***e.)** Hortense Spillers' "Women and Republican Formation", September, 2010; at Duke;*
***f.)** Gumbs, Alexis Pauline. Spill: Scenes of Black Feminist Fugitivity. United Kingdom: Duke University Press, 2016.*

[8]*a.) Karen C. Chambers Dalton, "The Alphabet Is an Abolitionist" Literacy and African Americans in the Emancipation Era; The Massachusetts Review Vol. 32, No. 4 (Winter, 1991), pp. 545-580; Published by: The Massachusetts Review, Inc.*
b.) Solayman Idris, Fugitive Intelligences : Orunage to Orionism, appended to The Sunrise in the West ; published by Lumifont Scriptorium for Nafura Nawra Buruj Miraj, 2019
c.) ADOS is merely a historically accurate term replaced by .the revelation of Orun.

[9]إِذِ ـمَا قَوْلُـنَا لِـشَـيْءٍ إِذَ ا أَر دْ نَـاهُ أَن نَـقُولَ لَـهُ كُن فَيِكُون *"When We will anything, We simply say to it 'Be!' and it is." -Surah al Nahl 16:40.*

2

Black matter
Forned + Shaped
by light
Cascades into
~~AAAAAAAAAAAAAA~~ real
Shatters into the
physical
Splinters into
Perception
Lost @ sunrise
Birthed @ dusk
Mediate Purple
Cradles and
~~Smothers~~ Us all

\
*
 o
 8
Salomé

\\

Would you love a secret wife?

///

Would you penetrate her 7 veils?

\\

And love her to the fullness of your passions?

///

...Conceal her in your heart...

\\\

Expose her in your gifts

//

*...Surely, She is the knowledge of **God**...*

\\\

Surely, She is a fickle mistress...

Aerolith & Black Box   (51:33)

```
                ******
               Aerolith
                  \
                  /
                  \
                  *
                                    ...Tears
    ~ ~ ~      ~ ~ ~   ( on High        )
       ~splash seas~    *                 *
     ) &
slay Dragons*....    Flaming ***)****
                                  ) swords;
                          *        guarding
       (                ) Eden )
      )*******...torching  *      *
Sodom*...
    ******* God's
       (            )******* Gifts *******
    fall *         *
    far:      (
               \
               /
               *
          Enlighten'
            Sky
             &
      ...[ EARTH ]...
```

5

Black Box   (105)

```
                \
              [*]
              /
               \
               *
_____ / \ _____
```

Heaven's   Kernel   ]

```
          /\      °      /\
                 \0/
                 ‘;’
                 \/

                  ن
```

Earth's   Navel
Squares   Circle
Centers   Cube
Humbles   Elephants

Glows   (.)   Light
Directs   Praise
Forgiving   sins
Looping   Pilgrims
Clothed   ن   White

Bathed   ن   Blood   ]

<u>Star Logic</u>

Oshun's Smile
Let there be light
Given Leave
in Darkness Embrace
Zodiac Daughter
Logged Orion's Belt

Heft of Breast
Balance of Scale
Curve of Hips
Loop of Ankh
Made fat by
Meteor Showers
Birthing Dominion
He's called forth
Dy Slaw Virgas
in Adorat
Like Summer, rivers

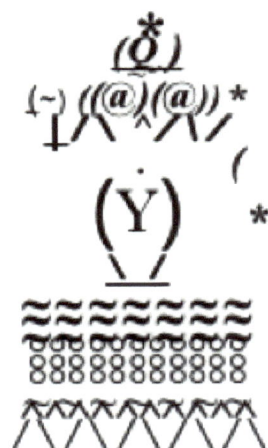

O   )   (76:17-18)

~salsabil~
Lightening strikes
Amidst nimbus
As moons dawn
Beneath black rainbows
Raven Rivers cascade
Honey dewed valleys
Gibraltars peak
Above brown egg
Pumpkin cushions
our royal lotus

8

O.G.sUS

First

of

Last

/Wonder * f Worlds\

Holy Mother

Joe Son

~

~ ~

~

Bout   Business

Live **%** Works

Rebukes   Wolves

Kisses   Traitors

Saves Neighbors

Slays   Haters

~   ~

Saturnalia

H
scholar
o
d

Charlie   chaseR

Root   man
Dope   Man
Pusher   Man
Crush   a Man
Rush   a man
Gush   a man
Chey   enne

♄

○

(4:1-3;
27:82)

Ursula

MoM   ma

Bear   With   bus

Stop   cubs

and   a   joey

in   pouch

Buys   snacks

Wipes   noses

&

scolds   bab   ies

"Sketches of Spain"[10]

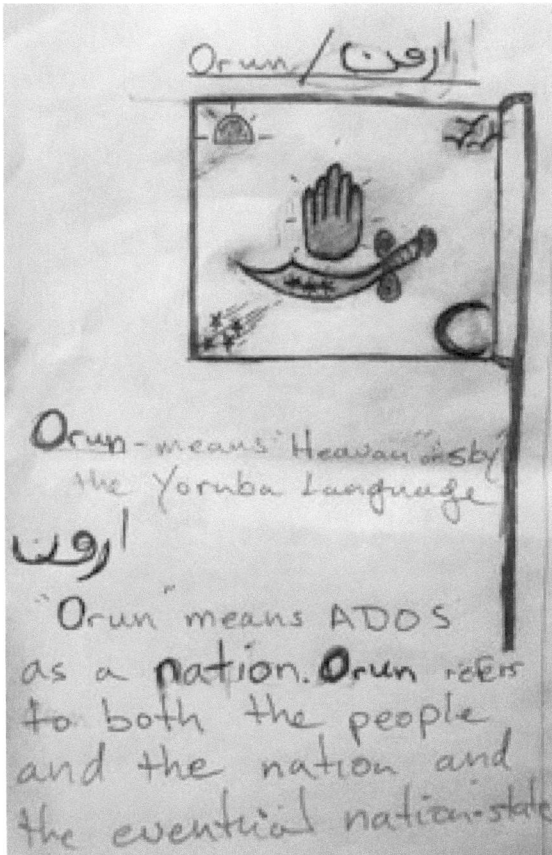

Orun / اِروۡرۡ (...)

Orun - means "Heaven" as by
the Yoruba Language
اِروۡن
"Orun" means ADOS
as a nation. Orun refers
to both the people
and the nation and
the eventual nation-state

---

[10]Miles Davis', "Sketches of Spain", album was inspired by the Afro- Arabic Moorish Kingdom of Andalusia,in Medieval Spain. Early conceptions of the Seal of Orun employed the Shriners Scimitar, representing Khalid bin Walid, known as (سَـــيۡف اللّٰه / Saif Allah) "the Sword of Allah".- Fahim A. Knight El, Freemasonry (Moslems Sons), and Islam: What do they Share , published by Fahim and Associates , Durham, N.C., 2005 . Whereas the seal of The Shrine has the sword facing from the West to the East; The Seal of Orun directs the Dhul Fiqr ذُو ٱلۡفَقَار towards The Sunrise in the West.

Orun Census Practice

On Sunday, August 16, 2020, a census worker, Janice, came to my home in Durham. My biblical aversion to census was only confirmed by the Covid crisis; reminding me of God's judgement of pestilence, against King David, for "numbering the people".[11] Taking heed to the the Word of the LORD, I recited Psalms 91[12] and did not mail my census form back.

When Janice came to my door, though, It was my intention to declare the Nation of Orun. I figured my declaring myself "Orun" would represent the acknowledgment of the First of Orun Nation, setting national precedent for the rest of ADOS.   My census declaration would represent the first "official" accounting of the

First Person: The Prime Element of the Orun Nation, The Kingdom of Heaven on Earth; at

---

[11] II Samuel, Chapter 24
Again the anger of the Lord burned against Israel. He moved David against them, saying, "Go, number Israel and Judah." 2 So the king said to Joab the captain of the army who was with him, "Go through all the families of Israel, from Dan to Beersheba. Number the people, so I may know how many there are."
I Chronicles, Chapter 21
Satan stood up against Israel, and moved David to number Israel. 2 So David said to Joab and the leaders of the people, "Go and number Israel from Beersheba to Dan. Then let me know how many people there are."

[12] Psalms 91 is understood to be the prayer of forgiveness, written by King David, as punishment for taking a census of Israel causing a plague that killed 70,000 men.

least as far as the U.S. government is concerned.[13] My engaging wouldn't be "the numbering of the people" of Orun, proper, so much as the *revelation* of The People of Orun : Our *Eclosure*. Understood as *Homo Sapiens Summa*[14], complete man; ALL humanity is becoming Orun; thus Orun Nation

---

[13] Christina M. Greer, Black Ethnics Race, Immigration, and the Pursuit of the American Dream, Oxford University Press, 2013

[14] **a.**)Solayman Idris, The Sunrise in the West, Lumifont Scriptorium for Nafura Nawra Buruj Miraj, Durham, N.C. 2019 Who is Orun & What is Orun, are chapters in The Sunrise in the West, defining Orun as Homo Sapiens Summa, Complete Humanity, and the eventual culmination of the Human Genome.
" ADOS and Orun differ in that ADOS are Orun before segregation and Orun is ADOS after desegregation and mingling and compiling the human genome. Shabazz, as in the "God Tribe" of the NOI, corresponds with Orun. Orun is Homo Sapiens Summa. Segregated society did not allow development into humanity's Prime Element."
"The "Divine Nation," Orun, are the primary ancestors and ultimate descendants of all humanity. ADOS, the current Orun Nation, also called Solar Orun, because slavery, success, and identity crises are mingled with all the nations of the world, recreating the complete genetic compilation of the originary Sun Tribe, who has until now been separated into different nations. Homo Sapiens Summa represents the proper speciation of Orun."
b.) Looking further into the characters of Orun and Orion, we might also note the Latin verb orior (rise, become visible) and its resonant constellation of cognates: origo (origin), oriens (east or orient, the direction of solar rising), and oriundus (about or needing to rise). - Dr. David Liu. Also, the Yoruba Orun, "Heavenly", correlates through the Arabic root a-r-n with the Persian Iran meaning "noble".

14

defies numbering[15] by virtue of it's ever expanding indefinite genomic composition. Orun Nation is the realized and realizing total Human Genome.

That day, I asked the Janice if she could check all the boxes. She tried but could not on her digital tablet. I then told her to put "Orun Nation" in the "other" space under ethnicity. She asked me what it meant and I said "It's all the peoples in the world, synthesized." Janice looked at me and said "Wow".

---

[15] Gen. 15:5 And he brought him forth abroad, and said, Look now toward heaven, and tell the stars, if thou be able to number them: and he said unto him, So shall thy seed be.

As soon as Janice entered the information, a Red Tailed Hawk[16] landed in the magnolia tree parallel to us on my balcony porch. A flock of birds in the tree began screaming and their cries were taken up by all the others, in the trees, cascading up the block, until the whole street was in screeching tumult. Janice said thank you and ran down the stairs in such a hurry that she forgot to get my downstairs neighbor's info, and had to come back up.

---

[16] a.) Religious beliefs and cognitive processes are in no way mutually exclusive. When the king was taken through the religious or "historical" situations to become the god Horus, e.g., the "Sacred Falcon," the identity King-Falcon could be conceived cognitively through a metaphorical extension initiating the movement from the "fetish-incarnation" level. Metaphor is used here as the conceptual tool through which the religious concept is materialized. This new "child of the mind" is now located in the religious sphere as a "godly manifestation." -Levi Strauss, Claude. The Savage Mind. United Kingdom: University of Chicago Press, 1966.
b.) During the activities giving birth to the particular metaphor "Falcon-King," the deep structure of the conceptual metaphor "Rulers Are Birds of Prey"43 has sired the interlacing of two separate domains: qualities such as speed, grace, sharp sight and predatory nature (and the like) have been borrowed from the falcon, whereas the human king has supplemented those sophisticated gestures feasible only for a human being. The fact that the Egyptians recognized and appreciated the abilities of the falcon can be deduced from the incarnation of the personificated [Horus] in a falcon form ("The falcon shows the regal aspects of command and perception of king or god" [Baines 1 985:65-6 with fig.65]) - Orly Goldwasser, From Icon to MetaphorStudies in the Semiotics of the Hieroglyphs(page 15); University of Virginia Press, Richmond, 1995

The birds screamed in chorus for a full five minutes before returning to regular conference.[17]

---

[17] a.)In the Qur'ān the term aṣ-ṣāffāt is taken as meaning literally the birds ,but as denoting symbolically the angels (al-malā'ikah); and thus…the constitution of the celestial or spiritual hierarchies…The word ṣaff or "rank," is one of those many words which have been suggested as the origin of the word ṣūfī and taṣawwuf; and although this derivation does not seem acceptable from a purely linguistic point of view, it is nonetheless true, as with many other derivations of the same kind, that it represents one of the ideas really contained in these terms: for the "spiritual hierarchies"are essentially identical with the degrees of initiation. - Rene Guenon, "The Language of the Birds", form "Symbols of Sacred Science", Sophia Perennis Press,1962
b.)"Shabazz" means "King Bird," "Eagle," or "Falcon" in Persian and Urdu; also the Simurgh of Persian literature"
c.) "Conference of Birds," published in 1177 by unknown authors.

17

The revelation of Orun Nation is ordained by the Most High and lauded by Creation.[18]

As the Holy Qur'an says,

قَدْ أَفْلَحَ الْمُؤْمِنُونَ

"Surely the believers are already successful."

We Praise The Most High for making Us successful in this most worthy of endeavors.

Amin.

---

[18]a.) Qur'an 27:16, Al Naml, "The Bee",

وَوَرِثَ سُلَيْمَانُ دَاوُودَ وَقَالَ يَا أَيُّهَا النَّاسُ عُلِّمْنَا مَنطِقَ الطَّيْرِ وَأُوتِينَا مِن كُلِّ شَيْءٍ إِنَّ هَذَا لَهُوَ الْفَضْلُ الْمُبِينُ

Solomon succeeded David. He said, 'People, we have been taught the speech of birds, and we have been given a share of everything: this is a clearly a great favour.'

b.) قَالَ رَبِّ اغْفِرْ لِي وَهَبْ لِي مُلْكًا لَا يَنبَغِي لِأَحَدٍ مِّنْ بَعْدِي إِنَّكَ أَنتَ الْوَهَّابُ

, "He said, "My Lord! Forgive me, and bestow upon me a kingdom such as shall not belong to any other after me. Verily, You are the Bestower."(Qur'an 38:35)23

c.) Surah 105 3-5, al Fil, "The Elephant,"

وَأَرْسَلَ عَلَيْهِمْ طَيْرًا أَبَابِيلَ 4. تَرْمِيهِم بِحِجَارَةٍ مِّن سِجِّيلٍ 5. فَجَعَلَهُمْ كَعَصْفٍ مَّأْكُولٍ

3. And He sent against them Flights of Birds, 4.Striking them with stones of baked clay. 5.Then did He make them like an empty field of stalks and straw, which has been eaten up.

d.) *see Section 1, "The Seal of Orun, Symbolic Lexicon: Conference of Birds" from The Sunrise in the West*

N

(*)
**Heavens
halo
Our heads
Around**

**Beyond
Our wants
lies
Love**
(˄)

**Within
Our Hearts
lives
Loss**
(o)

W

**Below
our legs
swells
Hell...**
(y)

$

Operational Guidance[19]

******* *ORU.N. Mandate, given by The Verdant Lady, Herself, gives authoritative responsibility, superseding organizational affiliation. With specific exception, Orun School as revelation, necessarily stands outside, above & beyond, and at the center of contemporary initiatic hierarchy.*[20]

***** *ORU.N. Nation calls for representation via a representative for inclusion in the Sovereign Nations, domestic and international governing bodies of the United States of America, the African Union and the United Nations; giving the right to take action and factor in determining domestic, global and world decision making relative to international policy and law.*

***** *ORU.N. is not a paramilitary organization nor is it a subversive radical or militant movement rooted in the objectives of treason or sedition against the United States Government or any other, nor is it in alliance with any international nations, movements, or organizations that advocate such.*

***** *ORU.N. is a law abiding organization geared towards ending and eradicating internal domestic violence, in the United States, amongst various street "Nations", that has proliferated into all manner of social discord.*

***** *ORU.N. is a nonviolent organization, possessing solutions and ideals, working to collectively solve the five centuries of problems, plaguing American Descendants of Slavery, in the Western hemisphere.*

---

[19]Excepting The First, these declarations were recommended by Baba Fahim A. Knight-El; Freemasonry (Moslem Sons) and Islam: What Do They Share? and Black Islam: 360° Knowledge , Wisdom, and Understanding, 2021. See Appended "Black Coffee Science"

[20] *Mandate & Prophetic Masonic Islam, The Sunrise in the West, 2019*

```
                          )
                          *

                          (                    (17:15—21;
                          *                     55:55-57;
                                                78:33-34)
                     zanjabil


                       * )

~~~(****genIe~~)~~~°^^°~~)~~~~sIster****)~~~
~(~~~~~~~~~~~~~*~~~~~~~~~~*~~(~~~~~~~~~~~~~~
    ~~*(~~~~~~~~~~~~~~~~~**~~~~*~~~~~~~~~
*(~~~~~~)~~~~~~~~~~egg Eyed ~~~~~~~~~~~~~~
   *(~~~*~~~~~~~°°°(***OasiS'***)°°°~~~~~~~~~
 **°°°*~*~*~*~*~(*~calyx~*)~*~*~*~*°°°**
  ~~~~~~'pear *^°~*_^°~*breasts'~~~~~~
                      *
                     **
                 shimmer'
                  flesh
                    ~
                    &
  ginger°°°°ᴧᴧᴧᴧᴧᴧ̃°°°°breath
   6 9*********************left
  XXXXXXXXXXXXXXXXXXXXXX
```

21

Orun Party Political Ritual I

On the Fourth of July, Veterans Day, Memorial Day, Juneteenth, and to inaugurate Black August,[21]

[21] **a.)** Black August began in California's San Quentin Prison in August 1979. The men who founded the holiday wished to commemorate the rich, tragic history of prison protest over the past decade as well as the number of historically significant events in the black freedom struggle that have taken place in the month of August... In a kind of secular activist Ramadan, Black August participants refused food and water before sundown, did not use the prison canteen, eschewed drugs and boastful behavior, boycotted radio and television, and engaged in rigorous physical exercise and political study. Through Black August, prisoners sought to demonstrate the personal power they maintained despite incarceration...For the founders, the month of August was also significant for tragic reasons. In 1971 imprisoned intellectual and Black Panther George Jackson was killed in a bloody uprising. His seventeen-year-old brother, Jonathan, had been killed the previous August attempting to free three prisoners from a Marin County courthouse. On August 1, 1978, Jeffrey Khatari Gaulden was killed during a game of touch football in the San Quentin prison yard. These events caused an already tense prison system to crack down on prisoner access to media and to the public. Their subversive study groups became more clandestine, as violence among prisoners and between prisoners and guards increased in frequency. And those who wished to press for social change from inside the prison faced steeper obstacles to participating in political organizations...[In addition to these 20th Century realities]There were slave rebellions, from the beginning of the Haitian Revolution (August 21, 1791) to those attempted by Gabriel Prosser (originally scheduled for August 30, 1800), launched by Nat Turner (beginning August 21, 1831), and called for by Henry Highland Garnett (August 22, 1843). There were deaths (W.E.B. Du Bois, August 27, 1963) and births (Marcus Garvey, August 17, 1887; Garvey's organization, the Universal Negro Improvement Association, formed in August 1914).-[Web Document] From Freedom Summer to Black August: Why Civil Rights Activists Should Champion a Little-Known Prisoner Holiday by Dan Berger August 19, 2014 *bracketed comments are mine
b.) *Verdieu, Gloria. Black August: 1619-2019. United States: Independently Published, 2019.* **c.)** ***Black August in the Park*** *is an annual celebration of these events held in Durham, N.C. founded by Moses Ochola, Chrystal Taylor, Joshua Gunn, Derrick Beasely, and Janelle Henry in 2016*

Orun Party burns confederate flags.[22] We perform this political ritual, in public and private, to commemorate Orun ancestors' burning plantations, sacrificing their enemies as black soldiers in the Union Army, during the Civil War.[23] nearly 400,000 Orun Soldiers joined the Union Army, slaying Confederate Masters; fighting and giving critical intelligence to Harriet Tubman, Frederick Douglas, Abraham Lincoln, and Ulysses Grant, among others; in exchange for land, guns, suffrage, and the right of return to Africa.[24]

Orun Civil War Veterans made covenant and sacrifice, to create Orun State, with the American government, during and immediately after the Civil War. Orun Nation was hidden, first: submerged with our ancestors, executed and lost,

---

[22] Orun Party participated in The Confederate Flag: A Belated Funeral project, with Professor Will Boone, Mixed Media Specialist, Malcom Goff, and Others, on Memorial Day, 2015, as N.C. representatives in the coordinated Lit Dixie, rebel flag burning, that took place in 13 states. In addition, Orun School consulted with John Sims on his The Confederate Flag Burn & Bury Support Kit project, YouTube video, Published on June 28, 2015, https://www.youtube.com/watch?v=wTrf0LJdDhU&fbclid=IwAR1i6bVxUl-Jsb5xmHKj2APQ9dFJJrTkppwV66-fH5HB-3nNr0DL7FMz9sM

[23]**b** .)James Henry Gooding, On the Altar of Freedom: A Black Soldier's Civil War Letters from the Front, ed. Virginia M. Adams, University of Massachusetts Press, April 6, 1999.

[24] **a.)** Thavolia Glymph, 'Between Slavery and Freedom': Rethinking the Slaves' War, NMAAHC/AHA Conference: The Future of the African American Past, Washington, DC, 19-21 May 2016.

en ba dlo, "beneath the waves"[25], in the middle passage, and suppressed on land, in other U.S. slave revolts[26]and population managements. Orun Nation and Orun State were to be revealed and realized immediately after the Civil War, but were eclipsed by racist terror and political witchcraft, using Jim Crow lynchings, targeting Orun Civil War Veterans, as blood sacrifices,[27] for white supremacist interests. Now manifest as police killings, these diabolical historical psycho-traumatic processes are relived and magnified via social media.[28]

---

[25] en ba dlo, meaning "beneath the waves," in French Creole is the Haitian Voodoo term for the spirit world; as the abode of those Orun who died during the middle passage.

[26]Maggie Montesinos Sale, The Slumbering Volcano American Slave Ship Revolts and the Production of Rebellious Masculinity, Durham, NC: Duke UP, 1997.

[27] Donald G. Matthews, The Southern Rite of Human Sacrifice: Lynching in the American South; The Mississippi Quarterly, Vol. 61, No. 1/2, Special Issue on Lynching and American Culture (Winter-Spring 2008), pp. 27-70. Baltimore, Maryland, Johns Hopkins University Press

[28] *Solayman Idris, "Orunage to Orionism": Reparations as Repatriation & Repatriation as Religion"* appended to *The Sunrise in the West,* Lumifont Scriptorium, Durham, N.C., 2019
b.) Understood as blood sacrifice, police shootings and their regular rebroadcast with consumption can be executed as sympathetic magic ritual accomplished on the populace.

According to Orun School Star Logic[29], both Orun Nation and Orun State's inception and birth, succeed one another, as Orun Meteor Time initiates the Later Solar Orun Age. The Leonid Meteor Shower of 1833, marks the coming of the Orun Nation[30] while the revolutionary founding of Orun State: latter Solar Orun Age, coincides with the arming and self defense of Orun Soldiers in 1863, during the American Civil War.[31] In the year 1866, American terrorist war was launched against Orun by the KKK.[32] The Kingdom of Heaven was active and present, but was eclipsed in the Nadir by Jim Crowe, and was not made

---

[29] **a.**) The term Star Logic comes from Anthony T. Browder, From the Browder File: 22 Essays on the African American Experience, published by The Institute of Karmic Guidance, Washington, D.C. 1989, chapter called A Brief History of Astrology and the United States.
b.) Solayman Idris, Star Logic (a collection of Poiesis), Durahm, N.C. 2020: published by Lumifont Scriptorium for Nafura Nawra Buruj Miraj

[30] Russel Thornton; Candess Greene., The Year the Stars Fell: The Smithsonian Winter Counts; Lincoln and London, University of Nebraska Press,2007. 2020 is the year 187-188, by Meteor Time.

[31] Solayman Idris, When is Orun? from The Sunrise in the West; Durham, N.C., Lumifont Scriptorium for Nafura Nawra Buruj Miraj, 2019.

[32] "W.E.B. Dubois, Black Reconstruction in the South: 1865-1877, New York: Harcourt, Brace & Co., 1935."

apparent.[33] Most recently, Orun Nation is revealed in part, under Orion Constellation, by 2019's Monoceros Meteor Shower, amongst other phenomena.[34] According to Star Logic, Orun School additionally tells time according to the succession of meteor showers, symbolic of Orun enlightenment, migration, resettlement, Intelligencia and Divine Retribution. The Union Army would not have won the Civil War without warriors and intelligence from Orun, that helped them rout the Confederates. Orun Intelligence and militancy was essential to the preservation of the Union and is the foundation of the new American democracy.[35] The "free world" owes the grandest debt to Orun Civil War Veterans *and kin.*[36] Orun Party Political Ritual necessarily commemorates these, among 0ther realities.

---

[33] 1866-1945, From Emancipation to Jim Crowe: A Glimpse of the Kingdom of Heaven: The Azuza Street Revival; PBS Documentary Series, 2003

[34] Solayman Idris, Symbolic Lexicon: Three Asterisks' note on Orion from The Sunrise in the West; Durham, N.C., Lumifont Scriptorium for Nafura Nawra Buruj Miraj, 2019

[35] Solayman Idris, The Sunrise in the West; Lumifont Scriptorium, Durham, N.C. 2019

[36]Thavolia Glymph, Disappeared Without Any Account Being had of Them: Enslaved Women and the Armies of the Civil War (Lecture) History of the Military, War, and Society Research Seminar Series. Durham, NC, Duke University, 29 October 2010.

Simone

Night Rider Riding

Broken Heart Abiding

Butterfly come out
of hiding

You know how I feel!

Orun Political Ritual Practice II: *We Be Us*

1. The *Lit Dixie:* Burning the Confederate flag, commemorates the lives and actions of Harriet Tubman, Haitian Revolutionaries, Nat Turner and Other American Slave Revolutionaries, along with Orun Civil War Veterans' burning of plantations, producing Our freedom. This can be done publicly or privately. As purchase of Rebel Flags is likely surveilled; Orun School recommends drawing Confederate flags on cardboard and setting the effigy on fire.

2. Regular communal Pilgrimage to the graves of African American leaders and martyrs, such as Harriet Tubman, El Hajj Malik Shabazz, Martin Luther King, Nat Turner, Fred Hampton Sr., Emmet Till, George Jackson and Others.

3. Regular community celebrations, like mentioned, annual *Black August In The Park* street festival in Durham, N.C. Celebrations should be held commemorating Harriet Tubman, the Haitian Revolution, George Jackson, Orun Civil War Veterans, Nat Turner, and Others. This can be done, in conscious expression, to prevent eclipse by distractivism and white supremacist spectacles.

4. Orun Census practice, begins in 2020, declaring ourselves an Ethno specific Orun nationality, written as *"Orun Nation"*, in the "Other" space. Writing Orun as nationality may be done with or without, any, and, or all, designations, marked, on the racial census, in preparation for eventual claims, to Our continental African nation state, Orun State. Orun does not ask that anyone give up their previous affiliations or designations. We only ask that, in addition to our historical titles, We now acknowledge that *We Be Us*.

5. We affix the attributes, *Orun* or *Ournullah* or simply the initial *"O"* as first middle or last names; beginning ethno specific naming and lineage, as revelation of Orun Nation, in preparation for eventual claims to Orun continental African nation state, Orun State.[37]

---

[37] a.) Frantz Fanon, *The Wretched of the Earth*, Paris France, Présence Africaine, 1963, writes "...the political parties, in order to show the nature of their action, which is all the same progressive. In their speeches the political leaders give a name to the nation. In this way the native's demands are given shape.
There is however no definite subject matter and no political or social program. There is a vague outline or skeleton, which is nevertheless national in form, what we describe as "minimum requirements..."
b.) "Orun's acceptance of "street tribe" nationality and operative initiative: establishing our continental African nation state, Orun State, can be seen as rendering most previous black nationalist sentiments and ideologies relatively speculatively obsolete. This would be untrue. Orun School necessarily builds upon these paradigms while achieving their goals in active capacity, while providing a litmus test for genuine Pan Africanist support, in the New an Old World for 'black liberation'." Orun School's use of Shabazz, Fanon, Cesaire, and Diop should further clarify these sentiments.

While these activities are not unique to Orun School, Our specific engagement, in these cultural ritual forms, strengthens the psychosocial bedrock of Orun national consciousness[38], via public and private, display and practice, of Our veneration of Orun Ancestors and Founders.

As the Holy Qur'an says,

قَدْ أَفْلَحَ الْمُؤْمِنُونَ

"Surely the believers are already successful."[39]

We Praise The Most High for making Us successful in this most worthy of endeavors.

Amin.

---

[38] a.) Eddleman, Murry, The Symbolic Uses of Politics; University of Illonois Press; Chicago, Illinois, 1985

b.) "The symbolic side of politics calls for attention, for men cannot know themselves until they know what they do and what surrounds and nurtures them. Man creates political symbols and they sustain and develop him or warp him."

c.) "Basic to the recognition of symbolic forms in the political process is a distinction between politics as a spectator sport and political activity as utilized by organized groups to get quite specific, tangible benefits for themselves."

d.) Orun School, Orun Party, and Orun Intelligencia are actively engaged in the analysis, formation, mobilization, and deployment of semiotic political ritual forms for the understanding, instantiation, and founding of Orun State.

[39] قَدْ أَفْلَحَ الْمُؤْمِنُونَ *Surat Al-Mu'minūn (The Believers), verse 1.*

Dei *pana*

Hand that Rocks
the Axis
Chief Lioness
Godess Priestess Princess
Mary Fatima
Morning Glory Dawn Chorus
Aurora's Sonrise
Oshun's semper
in Her Silver Mer
My Gracious Fate's Garment
spun of white Light Red Tie
Sister Nephys
Rejoin my Body
Bright Ishtar
Guide Me Forward
Write Our Story
Seshat Schola
Black Athena
Weigh our knowledge
Love Thy Neighbor Aphrodite
Slay our hate Kali Kali
Break our Fetters Lady Liberty
Kiss it Better Fairest Justice

```
          *

        (*)

         o
          .
         i
             *
         .
         i
              o
         *

            i
              .
              i
         *
            i
         *
         *  .
      i * i *
        *  i *
        *i*
          .
          i
       shish
       ‖‖‖
      Students
       stole
      heaven's
        Cult
        then
       taught
      Mystery
     as mirror
      Aromatic
      fetishes
      Workers
      toeked,
       Smiled
        then
      boogied
       Honey
      siphoned
      Stingers
      sheathed
      In heXXX
      palace
```

Alma Mater (6:143)

     *   *   *   *   *

   *   *   *

Noble Ma   *

Book's   *

              Recitals

     Sacred   ♈

     Pages'   *

              Peak   ♑

Eloquences'

            Epic   ♈

Cupidity's

            Fragrant

    Oases'

                    Paths'

Power   **Lord's**

                    Song

          of   **Five**

Rings   **of**

   War   **Art**

~Reap~ (3:185;34:14)

```
 *xxx*********************************************
 *ooooo
        xxxxxxxxxxxxxxxxxxxxxxxxxxxxxxxxxxxxxxxxxxxxx
< °######## oooooooooooooo********∧∧∧∧########
```

XX
Why
run
away
Death
xxloves
xxfear
xBows
xxXbe
xXfore
mar
tyrs
Avoids
x~thri~
x~vals
Murd
Xered
XXby
birth
XXX
XXX
XXXX

Chrysalis
_

what is

Our grave?

abode of death?

necropolis' Lot? plot

in The Reap3er's field?

Anubis' weigh station?

salt water tank for

Mothers? cocoon

for G. O.D.

<u>*moths*</u>

On Political Witchcraft:
Corporate Military Elite Sorcery
As Black Population Manipulation

The term *Star Logic* comes from *The Browder Files* chapter called "A Brief History of Astrology and the United States".[40] This chapter discusses the zodiacal significance of many holidays, political rituals and symbols such as voting , the Fourth of July, and the number 13. A later conversation, about presidents and statesmen who'd died on the Fourth of July[41] further cemented my view that certain aspects of statecraft, are occult practice, that I term "political witchcraft".

I'd the pleasure of meeting Russel Thornton, who'd co-authored *The Year the Stars Fell*,

---

[40] Anthony T. Browder, From the Browder File: 22 Essays on the African American Experience, published by The Institute of Karmic Guidance, Washington, D.C. 1989

[41] It is a fact of American history that three Founding Father Presidents—John Adams, Thomas Jefferson, and James Monroe —died on July 4, the Independence Day anniversary.

after a lecture in 2013.[42] I asked him about what I termed "political cannibalism": the slaughter of Natives, and then enshrining states, cities, and counties in their names. For instance, how many Lakota live in Dakota, or Manhattans in Manhattan? Russel told me, that according to Lakota practice, "political cannibalism", was a particularly malefic act that actually stole the soul, of a person or people; by slaying them, and taking their names and wearing their emblems, in addition to occupying their land(s).[43]

These practices of death and displacement along with the mass sacrifice of slaves and natives cultivate the infernal elements of American statecraft. I was forced to wonder: What are these former and current corporate military elites gaining by doing these horrific things? and furthermore what are they gaining by operating at these specific times?*

---

[42] Russell Thornton, A Rosebud Reservation Winter Count, circa 1751-1752 to 1886-1887 Ethnohistory (2002) 49 (4): 723–741 Duke University Press.
The Year the Stars Fell: The Smithsonian Winter Counts edited by Russel Thornton and Candess Greene, University of Nebraska Press, Lincoln and London, 2007

[43] Greg Johnson, *Narrative Remains: Articulating Indian Identities in the Repatriation Context;* Comparative Studies in Society and History Vol. 47 No. 3 (July 2005)Cambridge University Press

Nat Turner's Revolt[44] and The Haitian Revolution[45] began, August 14th and 21st, respectively. There were slave rebellions attempted by Gabriel Prosser (originally scheduled for August 30, 1800), and called for by Henry Highland Garnett (August 22, 1843). There were deaths (W.E.B. Du Bois, August 27, 1963) and births (Marcus Garvey, August 17, 1887) around the same auspicious time. Marcus Garvey's organization, the

---

[44] Nat Turner's Rebellion began in South Hampton County, Va. on August 21, 1831. Released, after his execution, The Confessions of Nat Turner, the Leader of the Late Insurrection in Southampton, Va. as fully and voluntarily made to Thomas R. Gray (1831), quote him as saying, "Spirit revealed to me the knowledge of the elements, the revolution of the planets, the operation of tides, and changes of the seasons...And on the appearance of the sign, (the eclipse of the sun last February) I should arise and prepare myself, and slay my enemies with their own weapons. And immediately on the sign appearing in the heavens, the seal was removed from my lips, and I communicated the great work laid out for me to do."

[45] a.) The Haitian revolution was initiated by the political ritual slaying of a pig, representing the impending massacre of whites on the island, by Boukman Dutty and Cecile Fatiman in Bois Cayman, August 14, 1891. On August 21, the revolution began in Port Au Prince, the capital city of San Domangue.
b.) See also, Solayman Idris, Qur'anic Poetics of Black Republicans: Afro Arabic Sources of Haytian Constitutionalism, appended to The Sunrise in the West: Lumifont Scriptorium, 2019, Durham, N.C.

Universal Negro Improvement Association, formed in August 1914.[46]

August 14, 2017 was the final day of the Perseid Meteor Shower, while the Cygnid Meteor shower began on August 17th ending on the 25th.[47] Auspiciously, it was also the weekend of a grand Solar Eclipse. Non coincidentally, it was also the same weekend of the now infamous mass White Nationalist demonstration, in Charlottesville, Virginia; when thousands of white supremacists, some carrying red Klan Crosses,[48]

---

[46] a.) Between August 7 and 28, Mars leads Jupiter and Saturn in transition between the constellations of Orion and Perseus (sword upraised, holding Medusa's head,   Ras Al Ghul, performing a celestial coup de tat) at sunrise, in the southern hemisphere. The relationship between the planet Mars and the star Ras Al Ghul, Jupiter and Saturn, Perseus and Orion, are worthy of a studies all their own. See   Black August Persian Perseus illustration, page V. b.) From Freedom Summer to Black August: Why Civil Rights Activists Should Champion a Little-Known Prisoner Holiday by Dan Berger August 19, 2014c.) Verdieu, Gloria. Black August: 1619-2019. United States: Independently Published, 2019.

[47] *The Perseids (007 PER) Jul 17–Aug 24, were most visible Aug 12 while the κ-Cygnids (012 KCG) Aug 03–Aug 25, were most visible on Aug 17 according to the International Meteor Organization   2017 Meteor Shower Calendar compiled by J¨urgen Rendtel1*

[48]   Becky Little, How Hate Groups are Hijacking Midieval Symbols Without knowing the Facts Behind Them, Documentary[Web Document], The History Channel, History .com, December 18, 2018 https://www.history.com/news/how-hate-groups-are-hijacking-medieval-symbols-while-ignoring-the-facts-behind-them

openly demonstrated in the streets, wreaking havoc, wearing regalia and matching khaki suits, carrying torches through the night.*White supremacist James Alex Fields mowed down leftist counter protestors with a car; killing one woman, injuring 19 people. In response to this demonstration, leftists staged the first of dozens of confederate monument desecrations and topplings, beginning on August 24, 2017, in my hometown, Durham, North Carolina. Since then, on the anniversary of the monument toppling, "progressives" attempt to take similar action.

In light of "The Browder Files", it was no coincidence to me, that whatever hidden hand was lighting the tiki torches, planned the white supremacist protest, on the Anniversaries of the Haitian Revolution and Nat Turner's Revolt.[49] This was done in part, to divert the powers of astrological convergence, that these Anniversaries, in concert with the Black August 2017 Solar Eclipse and meteor showers, would have had on the psycho social spectrum, of western blacks; consciously or *supra* consciously. On the Night of

---

[49]a.) Louis P. Nelson and Claudrina Howard, Charlottesville 2017: The Legacy of Race and Inequality, University of Virginia Press, 2018*

b.)Solomon Burnette, Yokel Critiques of Interstate Violence and Resistance [Web Document], Durham N.C.; published by The Clarion Content, August 23, 2017.
http://clarioncontentmedia.com/2017/08/yokel-critiques-of-interstate-racial-violence-and-resistance/

August 25, 2020; on the tail and front cusps of the Perseid and Cygnid meteor showers; 17-year-old, Kyle Rittenhouse, shot two protestors with an AR15, at a Black Lives Matter rally[50], in Kenosha Wisconsin. Rittenhouse was allowed to traipse past officers with a gesture and a nod after laying down two men with a long gun. We all watched in disbelief and dismay on social media as the police seemingly ignored Kyle's raised hands as he walked by, until he dropped them and continued on his way.[51]

Once again, on the auspicious eves of ancestral revolutionary efforts and victories, American Blacks were fed stories of victimhood, and and led in ineffectual protest by whites. Many left off meditation on ancestral struggle, in lieu of manufactured rally and vandalism. Right Wing supremacist, and Left Liberal distractivists, once again, diverted collective consciousness; psychosocially manipulating our civilization and discontents. Counter Intelligence Programmers don't have to worry about what you think, if

––––––––––––––––––––

[50] *a.)17-year-old arrested in killing of 2 people in Kenosha by MIKE HOUSEHOLDER and SCOTT BAUER Associated Press Wednesday, August 26th 2020*
b.)Kyle Rittenhouse found not guilty after fatally shooting two in Kenosha unrest Maya Yang and Joanna Walters Fri 19 Nov 2021 15.36 EST
*see 2021 Meteor Calendar appended to this volume

[51] understood as blood sacrifice, police shootings and their regular rebroadcast with consumption can be executed as sympathetic magic ritual accomplished on the populace.

they've already surveyed your horizon, initiated a scenario for you, and have measures in place.

All the same, as far as planning goes, there's no way to operate against intuitive adaptability of Orun epigenetic activated 'ancestral' or 'celestine' intelligence.[52] Thus, the Corporate Military Elites' (CMEs) game is to prevent Star Logic activation via population management programs, in the long run; utilizing distractivist sleight of hand and white supremacist spectacle, in the short term. In essence, if you look at the shiny thing, you don't think about the deep thing. At least, not at the critical moment. Diabolical astrological dialectics and redirection are a large part of the CMEs' political witchcraft during Black August, regarding Orun Nation, in the Western Hemisphere.

Going back to that summer day, in Durham, August 14, 2017; in light of the Solar Eclipse, Nat and Hayti's anniversary, the meteor showers, and Charlottesville rally; I immediately drew a Confederate Flag and set it on fire with my homie outside our apartments. I did this in commemoration of Nat Turner, Haitian Revolutionaries, Harriet Tubman, slave rebels and

---

[52]

بِسْمِ اللهِ الرَّحْمَنِ الرَّحِيمِ

وَإِذْ يَمْكُرُ بِكَ الَّذِينَ كَفَرُوا لِيُثْبِتُوكَ أَوْ يَقْتُلُوكَ أَوْ يُخْرِجُوكَ وَيَمْكُرُونَ وَيَمْكُرُ اللهُ وَاللهُ خَيْرُ الْمَاكِرِينَ

Surah al Anfal "The Spoils of War" 8:30 *Remember how the Unbelievers plotted against thee, to keep thee in bonds, or slay thee, or get thee out (of thy home). They plot and plan, and Allah too plans; but the best of planners is Allah*

42

Orun Civil War Veterans setting fire to plantations. I was conscious, then, that if white supremacist interests, were orchestrating ceremonial demonstrations and riotous distractivisms, on the left *and* the right, to divert Orun radical potential; then Orun political ritual, by comparison, is formulaically, righteously, exponentially, all the more magnified in power, by just cause, in purpose, impact, and aftermath.[53]

In subversion of this principal, most if not all American protest movements and media events, at least since the 2017 Solar Eclipse, occurring in and around Black August: be they white supremacist protests, leftist statue toppings, iconic tragedies, or electoral posturing are misdirection:

---

[53] **a.)** The current trend in confederate monument toppling also began that weekend, in Durham, N.C. representing leftist attempts to garner the synergies from the moment also. It seemed so orchestrated. It seemed like whites were using distractivism to keep ADOS's collective consciousness from contemplating Nat Turner and the Haitian Revolution during a Solar Eclipse. **b.)** "…The recent Solar Eclipse [August 21, 2017] marked the anniversary of Nat Turner's revolt in Southampton CountyVirginia and this week the Haytian Revolution began. These auspicious occasions should be reverenced by diasporic people, lest we forget. On the low, these historic moments are probably what spurred the supremacists to march in Virginia when they did. Never mind them statues, get in tune…"- Solomon Burnette, Yokel Critiques of Interstate Violence and Resistance [Web Document], Durham N.C.; published by The Clarion Content, August 23, 2017. http://clarioncontentmedia.com/2017/08/yokel-critiques-of-interstate-racial-violence-and-resistance/

sleight of hand, meant to divert ADOS' attention, from possible Orun supra conscious epigenetic 'ancestral' intelligence activation.[54]

Turning Frantz Fanon's psychoanalytic lens to Orun, we can see the siphoning and redirection of ADOS' (non) violent revolutionary potentia, away from community self empowerment ideals, towards focus on white supremacist spectacles such as the Charlottesville Protest and Rittenhouse's 2020 shooting. Distractivist leftist iconoclastic toppling of confederate monuments directs angst towards bought and paid for properties. The political posturing of the President and congress trickles down to support of either side of the always destructive, sometimes deathly, riotous, theatre. A plethora of music festivals and sports events ("food and games") are always planned around these auspicious stellar occasions.

From *The Wretched of the Earth* we can understand the many ways that colonizers reroute native revolutionary energies from the 1950s until now. Benighted and exacerbated by global corporate military elite diobolique planning and design; We must keep in mind, that contemporary "Black on Black violence", in large part, is psychotraumatic aggressions, meant for society's grand oppressors, taken out our (y)our own

---

[54] "Jacobs Eugenics", appendix to The Sunrise in the West, 2019

people.[55] While there indeed was lethal violence recorded among slaves; during slavery until emancipation, black social violence was largely directed outward, against whites, property, slave owners and colonialists. Certain maroon practices chrystalize this understanding.[56]Liberating human impulses and *will to freedom* had and have celestial spurs and correspondences. The Black August slave revolts took place with Mars leading stately Jupiter and Saturn in Sagittarius, transitioning between Orion and the Perseus constellation, at sunrise; mythologically carrying, the *Ras Al Goul,*

---

[55] Frantz Fanon, The Wretched of the Earth, Paris France, Présence Africaine 1963, Towards an African Revolution, 1964, and A Dying Colonialism, Monthly Review Press,1965.

[56] Helen McKee , "From Violence to Alliance: Maroons and White settlers in Jamaica, 1739–1795,Pages 27-52 | Published online: 20 Jun 2017 Download citation https://doi.org/10.1080/0144039X.2017.1341016

45

star in "The Spectre's 's Head"[57], performing a stellar coup de tat on Medusa. This celestial dynamism symbolized slave masters and the corporate military elites, impending massacre and

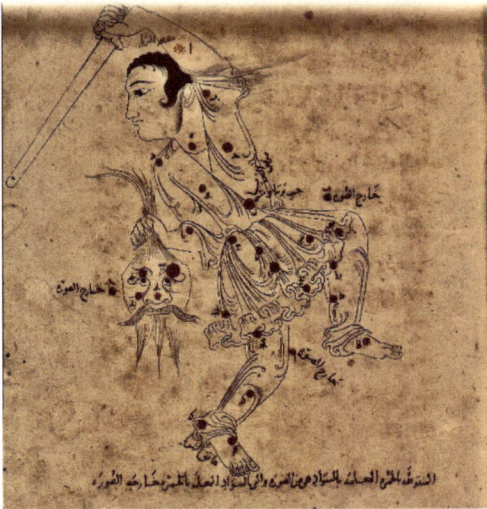

[57] **a.** Between August 7 and 28, Mars leads Jupiter and Saturn in transition between the constellations of Orion and Perseus (sword upraised, holding Medusa's head, Ras Al Ghul, performing a celestial coup de tat) at sunrise, in the southern hemisphere. The relationship between the planet Mars and the star Ras Al Ghul ,Jupiter and Saturn, Perseus and Orion, are worthy of a studies all their own.. **b.** Briefly about this particular star of legend, "With astronomical writers of three centuries ago Algol was **Caput Larvae,** the Spectre's Head... the **Head of Medusa...** The Chineese gave [the star] the gruesome title **Tseih She,** the Piled-up Corpses..." -Richard Hinkley Allen, Star Names: Their Lore and Meaning; Dover Publications, NY, NY 1963 is an unabridged and corrected republication of the work first published by G.E.Stechert in 1899 under the name Star Names and Their Meanings.
Black August Persian Perseus`-Abd Al Rahman Al Sufi; The Book of Fixed Stars; 964;correcting Ptolemy's Al Magest 147 CE

46

overthrow.[58] In the immortal words of Orun Warriors, *Sic Semper Evello Mortem Tyrannis,*.[59]

Whites greatest fear in the new world has always been slave revolts.[60] Political witchcraft comes into play when whites, upon recognizing the stellar patterns of slave revolts, undertake torturous sadistic sacrificial pains, to ensure that the persons and environmental ingredients needed to recreate these events, if only educationally, are not remembered or replicated. Thus, what had previously been externalized impulses have to be rendered inert, repressed, or better yet, for

---

[58] **a.)** THE SACRIFICIAL RITUALS OF GREEK HERO-CULTS IN THE ARCHAIC TO THE EARLY HELLENISTIC PERIOD by Gunnel Ekroth, University de Liege Press, 2002 **b.)**"Master of the Wood: Moral Authority and Political Imaginaries in Haiti" by Greg Beckett; Political and Legal Anthropology Review Vol. 27, No. 2 (November 2004), pp. 1-19, American Anthropological Association **c.)** See Black August Persian Perseus illustration

[59] **a.)** "Thus always I bring death to tyrants."- Marcus Junius Brutus; said before stabbing Caeser. Before it was used by John Wilkes Booth after shooting Abraham Lincoln, it was the State motto of Virginia, its shortened form, Sic Semper Tyrannis (Thus always to tyrants) . **b.)** Sic Semper Tyrannis was also the motto of almost 200,000 Orun Civil War Veterans, known as the United State's Colored Troops((USCT), who were Active May 22, 1863 – Oct 1865 and were Disbanded October 1865 as part of the Union Army comprising infantry, cavalry, artillery, and engineering MOS'. The 175 regiments hosted 178,000 men in the American Civil War- Of note on this topic is the text by William Gladstone, United States Colored Troops, 1863–1867. Gettysburg, PA: Thomas Publications, 1996.

[60] Laurent Dubois, *Avengers of the New World*, Belknap Press, 2005.

population management, turned inward *into black on black violence.*[61] Black on Black violence; in concert with the epic amorality of deculturization; is produced by a matrix of super structural factors, beyond ADOS' control, that exacerbate epigenetic trauma responses, into ever escalating prolonged violent conflicts. The planning and design of these repressions, is actually geopolitical and takes time and money, and spans the globe.[62]

Under the Taliban in Afghanistan, opium production had dropped 90%. After the U.S. take over, poppy production shot through the roof.[63]The increase in opium production led to a surplus. The surplus created an enhanced black market trade. These surplus, black market, war on terror opiates, get dumped into black communities, causing gang wars.[64]

---

[61] Frantz Fanon, The Wretched of the Earth, Paris France, Présence Africaine, 1963, Towards an African Revolution, 1964, and A Dying Colonialism, Monthly Review Press,1965.

[62] **a.)**Frantz Fanon, The Wretched of the Earth, Paris France, Présence Africaine, 1963, Towards an African Revolution, 1964, and A Dying Colonialism, Monthly Review Press,1965. **b.)** Vittoria, Stephen., Abu-Jamal, Mumia. Murder Incorporated - Dreaming of Empire: Book One. United States: Prison Radio, 2018.

[63] *"Opium Wars", National Geographic* [Web Document] https://www.nationalgeographic.com/magazine/2011/02/opium-wars/

[64] Dope inc. : Britain's Opium War against the U.S by Konstandinos Kalimtgis edited by Executive Intelligence Review (1978-08-06) Paperback – January 1, 2010

On the other hand, *legal* poppy surplus initiated a culture of medical professional overprescription, and an expanded market was created to push the war on terror legal prescription opiates. Hip Hop music was employed to market the dope, because opiate use had been frowned upon during the 90s through the 2000s. Rap music can make anything stylish. After American society was allowed to degenerate from the subsequent mass addictions, an "Opioid Crisis" was declared, and Corporate Military Elites (CMEs) now get to pay themselves to clean up the very mess, that they created domestically, with the invasion of Afghanistan. Police, hospitals, Social Services, civilian contractors, and the Military all get a boost. Everyone but addicts.

CME diabloliques eat off of the legal and illegal international drug trade, every step of the way, from the importation, to taxing rappers, to law enforcement, to the immediate health care and long term treatment responses. Networked with astrological considerations, 2012's burning of 500 Qur'ans in Afghanistan, and a war's worth of human sacrifice; it's some serious political witchcraft.[65] Most of us don't think that the kid stealing Percosets is a government employee, but he

---

[65] *"Diaboliques"* refers to predatory occultists in *Foucault's Pendulum* by Umberto Ecco, 1984 b.)CME:Piper, Michael Collins. *The High Priests of War: The Secret History of how America's 'neo-conservative' Trotskyites Came to Power and Orchestrated the War Against Iraq as the First Step in Their Drive for Global Empire.* American Free Press, 2004.

is, whether he knows it or not. If he decided to stop and go clean, the program that guided him out of his destructive addictive cycle, would have been conceived by the same intelligences who imported the opiates to begin with. It's all internationally sinister and lends itself to Orun population management domestically.

Orun School, recognizes the elemental nature of manipulated black on black violences, and takes as Our responsibility the negotiation of peace amongst the warring Nations and Sects; called the different Houses of Orun, by identifying and unifying with Black Fraternal Orders around the common cause of legitimization for the founding of Orun State.[66] Orun School sublimates ADOS' will to freedom, and counteracts political witchcraft by identification and institutionalization of Orun Political Ritual, among other modes, mobilizing Prophetic Biblical Afro Islamic literary formulae, in primary statecraft, for national recognition, *in earth as it is in heaven.*[67]

Knowledge is Power. These considerations and experiences answer in part, some questions that are pertinent to Orun School including: What are some aspects of political witchcraft? and How does Orun Party defend against it?

---

[66] The Sunrise in the West by Solayman Idris, published by Nature Nawra Buruj Miraj, Durham, N.C. 2019

[67] "Thy Kingdom Come, Thy will be done, In Earth as it is in Heaven", of the Lords Prayer is Orun

"…The G.O.D. left Lessons on my dresser…"
Ghostface Killah, *Can It All Be So Simple*, 1993

Hand of Fatimah/Benson - Universal symbol of peace/...

The flag represents repatriation, migration...

Shooting stars - intelligencia, angelic security + advent of a new age

Waxing moon representing drawing strength and guidance through Darkness

Sunrise, Orion - Prophet Muhammad (saw) ... said that in the last Day's, the Sun will Rise in the West. The Orion understand this as metaphor ADOS enlightenment + religion in the West. The Sun...

Dhulfiqar is a Universal symbol of Power, ... and the Rule of ... on the blade represent Orion's Belt.

ADOS as a people, as a nation, as a gathering, and as a sovereign nation state.

Sunrise, sky the ...

On ReNationalization

As a result of cultural erasure and denationalization, an Orun specific *renationalization* is necessary, in order for the formerly enslaved, to take the proper steps, for top tier (geo)political agendizing, organization, and institution building.[68]

Renationalization, as a primary goal of Orun School, has largely already been achieved in what is commonly called "Gang Culture". The Bloods, The Crips, The Folks, The Latin Kings, and some Black Muslims, among Others; all have specific "knowledges", literatures, signs & symbols, languages, rituals, ceremonies, scripts and territories, often based on intergenerational residence; and as such represent different "Nations". In light of these criteria, We All rightly refer to Ourselves as such.[69] The umbrella of Orun School, Orun Party, Orun State, Orun Nation, and Orun Intelligencia allow these different Houses of Orun to come together, under a common, benevolent, unifying cause, of grand

---

[68] Solayman Idris, The Sunrise in the West, Lumifont Scriptorium for Nafura Nawra Buruj Miraj; Durham, N.C., 2019

[69] A Political Analysis of Gangs: Potentialities, Subversions, Subornments, Speculation and Operation (Presented to panel of Community Artist, Activist, and Academics as part of a Team Service Project with Public Allies North Carolina, Durham, N.C., January 2009); Capstone project for Political Science Minor at North Carolina Central University 2009, under Professor Geoffrey Elliot(rip).

import and benefit, to the whole world:[70] The founding of Orun State.

Orun Party, takes renationalization for granted[71], to an extent, allowing Orun Intelligencia to reapply concentration, tacking between domestic and international concerns. Orun Intelligencia focuses energy stateside, on initiating and maintaining the Diya Peace,[72] in conversation and concert with the United Nations, and public-private partnership with American State and Other parties. Additionally, Orun Party engages the international community, in the Amer African Statecraft of planning, organizing, initiating and founding Orun State. Orun State is Orun People's continental African homeland Nation-State, reestablished, in part, by repatriation to land concessions made by the African Union, as

---

[70] Solayman Idris, The Sunrise in the West, Lumifont Scriptorium for Nafura Nawra Buruj Miraj, Durham, N.C. 2019

[71] "Critical and liberating dialogue, which presupposes action, must be carried on by the oppressed at whatever stage of their struggle for liberation"``- Paulo Frere, *Pedagogy of the Oppressed*

[72] ibid. "The Islamic practice of paying diyah, restitution, or "blood money", for a wrongful death or violation allows warring houses to work out peace deals rather than resorting to murder to settle disagreements. Diyah is often used by peacemakers and the United Nations to broker between tribes and nations in the middle east, Africa, Afghanistan, and Pakistan. La Cosa Nostra's practice of paying restitution comes from Sicilians, who were occupied by Moors for centuries."- For a more complete discussion diyah and negotiations see, The Sunrise in the West: Why is Orun?

reparations for continental African's historical role in the transatlantic slave trade.[73]

Orun fully acknowledges the contribution of the past political, cultural and social gains attributed to the sacrifices of our Black Power revolutionary warriors. In a sense, Orun School is neither Black Nationalist, nor is it Pan Africanist, though. It could only be conceptually understood as *Geo-Nationalist* in the literal sense, though that would make *Cielo-Nationalist* even more appropriate. Orun School necessarily and sufficiently carries Pan Africanist and Black Nationalist intents to their ultimate insular conclusions for ADOS. Orun's acceptance of "street tribe" nationality and operative initiative: establishing our continental African nation state; renders some previous black nationalist sentiments and ideologies speculatively obsolete. Orun School's use of Pan Africanist and Black Nationalist Theorists, such as Shabazz, Ture, Fanon, Cesaire, and Diop enhances these sentiments carrying them to their ultimate applications as pan africanist black nationalist

---

[73]   Solayman Idris, "Orunage to Orionism": Reparations as Repatriation & Repatriation as Religion" appended to The Sunrise in the West, Lumifont Scriptorium, Durham, N.C., 2019

agendas for ADOS.[74]   Orun School necessarily builds upon these paradigms while achieving their goals in active capacity; providing a litmus test for genuine Pan Africanist support, in the New *and* Old World, for 'black liberation'.   If our continental African Pan Africanist allies are sincere, they should begin immediately advocating in concert with Orun Party, in the United Nations, and the African Union, for the rightful recognition of Orun Party, Orun Nation, and the establishment of Orun State.[75]

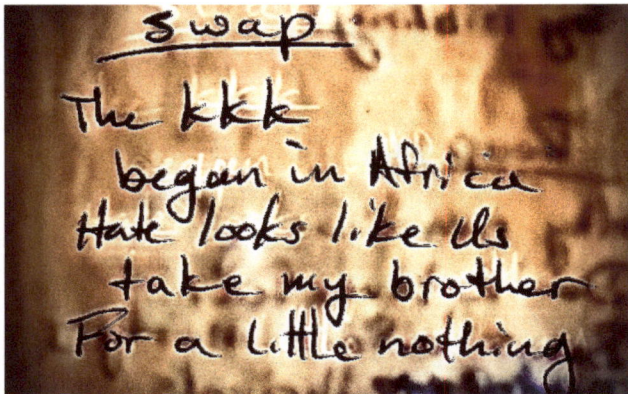

---

[70] a.)Frantz Fanon, The Wretched of the Earth, Paris France, Présence Africaine, 1963, Towards an African Revolution, 1964, and A Dying Colonialism, Monthly Review Press,1965.
  b.) Aimé Cesare, Discourse on Colonialism, Présence africaine 1955 c.) "Cheikh Anta Diop, The Africa Origin of Civilization: Myth or Reality, New York: L. Hill, 1974"

[75]For a more complete discussion on establishment of continental African Orun State, see "Orunage to Orionism": Reparations as Repatriation & Repatriation as Religion and F(0)unding Orun State, from The Sunrise in the West: Lumifont Scriptorium for Nafura Nawra Buruj Miraj, Durham N.C. 2019

Travail

****
****

```
                 Attack
         without          regard
      when               (         you
      are          )          *         low
      Call         *       (              for
    arbitration           *      When you
    gain on them                Humanity
  More or less.                 Unconscious
  of it's          )                    boon
   Turned sinister  *        by forgetfulness
     Stoney hearts        Making war on
      the garden Yea,  )  making war in
         our womb.  *        Spiritually
                 mis    carried
```

56

The Lit Dixie

I came into undergrad at 25 years old out of prison. I was a non traditional student and had already envisioned my curriculum and program of study. I'd a couple of setbacks, but in the end, I majored in European History at North Carolina Central University with a minor in Poli Sci and a concentration in International Relations. I focused on Andalusia, Moorish Spain, for my study and had to learn Arabic and Spanish. I studied Arabic at Duke via the inter-institutional program which is where I met Mbaye Lo,[76] Bruce Lawrence,[77] and Miriam Cooke.[78] They're gracious scholars, heavy heavy weights in Arabic and Islamic Studies, and invaluable contributors to Orun Intelligencia. I'd been studying Arabic in my cell in solitary and picked up Spanish from cholos on the yard. Carrying these skills forward allowed my transition into college life after prison easier.

My capstone project for my undergrad degree in European history was a study in Irish Republican Army symbolism, titled "Burning the Union Jack". I noted that the IRA uses "The Red

[76] Mbaye Lo, Muslims in America: Race, Politics and Community Building, Amana Publications, 2004.

[77] Bruce Lawrence, Islam Beyond Borders, Durham, NC: Duke University Press, 2016.

[78] Miriam Cooke, Tribal Modern: Branding New Nations in the Arab Gulf, University of California Press, 2014.

Hand of Ulster", which, at face value, could correspond to the Hand of Fatimah, as a primary symbol."[79] Discussion of the purple and red, right and left hands of Fatimah and Ulster do not denote any ties or connections between Sin Fein and Orun Party. As far as political escoterics go, in general, correspondent uses of hand symbolism across time and space; is worthy of attention and study.[80] The reverence for the Family of the Prophet, and use of the *Hamsa* is known beyond the AfroLatinoEuro spectrum of "black" and "white" peoples[81]. I want to state again clearly that this was purely an intellectual exercise and that there are no ties between Orun Party and Sen Fein.[82]

---

[79] René Guénon, "The Science of Hand-Reading in Sufism" ("La Chirologie dans l'ésotérisme islamique," Le Voile d'Isis, 289, 1932).
Steve Bruce, The Red Hand: Protestant Paramilitaries in Northern Ireland, Cambridge University Press, 1992

[80] William Leaf and Sally Purcell; *Heraldic Symbols: Islamic and Western Heraldry*; Victoria and AlbertMuseum, London; 1986

[81] Thomas Hylland Eriksen, Richard Jenkins; Flag, Nation and Symbolism in Europe and America: Routledge Taylor and Francis Publishing, London and New York, October, 2007

[82] ***** *ORU.N. is not a paramilitary organization nor is it a subversive radical or militant movement rooted in the objectives of treason or sedition against the United States Government, nor is it in alliance with any international nations, movements, or organizations that advocate such. - Operational Guidance #3*

The "Burning the Union Jack" project came about in large part, from a conversation with a classmate in 2008, outside our "Theories of Difference" in the Literature Department at Duke, taught by V.Y. Mudimbe, author of *The Invention of Africa: Gnosis, Philosophy, and the Order of Knowledge (African Systems of Thought)*[83]. The class was history of ideas: an existentialist epistemology of thought and writ; time-lining prevailing notions of constituted normal and pathological orders: using discourse, for inscribing and exscribing the Self and the Other, as in groups and out groups, eventually leading to the formation of nation(s) states, and enemy populations. The class was rich. I'm just now getting a lot of what we discussed. Sartre, Freud, *Maleaus Maleficarum*, Foucault, Fanon, and Canguilhem, were assigned readings among other literatures.

After "Theories of Difference" class, me an Homie were talking about recent American missile strikes over the Pakistani border, in the Afghanistan War. Pakistanis responded to this perceived breach of sovereignty, with protests in Karachi; burning effigies of George W. Bush.[84] Homie said, "Given

[83] V. Y. Mudimbe, The Invention of Africa: Gnosis, Philosophy, and the Order of Knowledge (African Systems of Thought), Bloomington, IN: Indiana UP, 1988.

[84] Katherine H. Adams, Michael L. Keene, Paper Dolls: Fragile Figures, Enduring Symbols, McFarland and Company, Inc. Publishers, Jefferson, N.C., 2017

that Pakistan is a nuclear power, we should be glad that they responded only in protest."

At that moment, creation of a figure of someone, and setting it on fire, struck me more as a potential magical practice as well a political one. Considering the "political witchcraft" of burning effigies, I said, "Wow, Dubya must have one hell of a headache." My peer responded, "Luckily he's protected by a magic oval." We laughed riotously... It was a fairly simple thought, but it lent itself to a different understanding of statecraft. It made me understand burning state symbols or "immolative iconoclasm" (and response) much differently. On a side note, the later burning of up to 500 Qur'ans, at Bagram Air Force base in Afghanistan, in 2012, should be understood as immolative political ritual witchcraft, also.[85] Back in 2008, I wanted to explore flag burning and iconic immolation as a serious study, but I didn't want to be taken as a terrorist sympathizer, a charlatan magi, or crackpot intellectual. I asked my advisors on how to frame it.

American flag burning discussions are passe. For Orun Party. Burning the Israeli flag; essentially just the Star of David, can be understood as

---

[85] Kristina Myrvold, The Death of Sacred Texts Ritual Disposal and Renovation of Texts in World Religions, Routlidge, Taylor and Francis Group, London and NY, 2016

counter productive to the grander goals of *Orionism*.[86]

In 2008, the burning Bush effigies, that sparked my contemplation, were too fresh, and I didn't want to be a war on terror sensationalist journalist. At that time, the Afghanistan conflict was very much televised. It was too much. This capstone project had to be historically sound, layered, and tight. My advisor, Carlton Wilson the Chair of the History Department at North Carolina Central University, had recruited me and was published on Afrocentrism in Europe.[87] I knew I had to be sharp.

I decided to look at the history of burning European national flags, in African and Carribbean decolonial protest, from a Fanonian lens. I wanted to use Fanon's psychoanalytics[88] to

---

[86] a.) That is not to say we do not critique and call for justice regarding the institution and maintenance of the Post Holocaust Resettlement Project called Israel. Orun finds the immolation of the Star of David, which is originally an Orun Hebrew symbol denoting royal affiliation with the Tribe of Judah, (an expression of Orun) to be distasteful, if not symbolically self destructive.
b.)"Orunage to Orionism": Reparations as Repatriation & Repatriation as Religion and F(0)unding Orun State, form The Sunrise in the West: Lumifont Scriptorium for Nafura Nawra Buruj Miraj, Durham N.C. 2019

[87] Lydia Lindsey and Carlton E. Wilson, *Spurring a Dialogue To Place the African European Experience Within the Context of an Afrocentric Philosophy*, Journal of Black Studies, Vol. 25, No. 1, Sep. 1994.

[88] Frantz Fanon, A Dying Colonialism, Monthly Review Press,1965 And Towards an African Revolution, 1964.

look at the burning of European colonial banners; not only representing decolonization of Africa, Asia, and the New World; but also as calling for, and prefiguring, the Destruction of *the whole* Metropole: the empire as well. The "Fall of Babylon"[89] of the Book of Revelation[90]; if you will. I was wowed by the thought.

I told Professor Wilson, expecting him to gush with pride. He listened to my bullet points during office hours and asked, "How is that European History?" Baffled, I said "I understand colonial history in many ways to be European History. Fanon was educated and wrote *Black Skin White Masks* in France. Perhaps engaging the Afro Caribbean European decolonial intelligencia should be folded in."[91] He said, "That's smart. That sounds like a book of African and Caribbean intellectual history. Regarding your reading of flag

---

[89] Nathaniel Samuel Murrell, William Spencer, Adrian Anthony McFarlane; Chanting Down Babylon:The Rastafari Reader, Temple University Press, Philadelphia, Penn., 1998

[90] a.) Revelation 14:8 "And there followed another angel, saying, Babylon is fallen, is fallen, that great city, because she made all nations drink of the wine of the wrath of her fornication.
b.) Bablyon in the symbolic sense, has been applied to London, New York, Washington D.C., and Paris in European Christian, religious black nationalist and pan africanist eschatologies.

[91] Odile Cazenave, Patricia Célérier, Contemporary Francophone African Writers and the Burden of Commitment; University of Va. Press, Richmond, 2011

burning as prefigurative immolative metropolitan symbolism, representing the burning of the capital city, in the Afro Caribbean context; It can be understood more properly as predictive of Europe's future, rather than its history, in a sense. This *Babylon thing*; it's prophecy." I blinked.

Continuing, he put me on further. Guiding my study, He reminded me that "European nationality is a construction of compiled ethnicities into empires, protectorates, kingdoms, and eventual states." He added, "Europeans colonized at home before they colonized abroad. Their own people burned their flags before anyone else did." He reminded me that, "European dissident groups generally consider themselves separate nationalities or ethnicities, and regularly take it upon themselves to immolate or torch state symbols. A European history project, following your train of thought, Solomon, need focus on inter European colonization and protest. Since Fanon is usually used for analyzing Caribbean and African contexts, applying Fanon in the domestic, insular, European context could be provocative.[92]I would be interested in reading that. Tighten your scope. Find a specific case and focus on it."

It was a fairly simple pruning. It taught me so much though. This is how I ended up studying

---

[92] Lydia Lindsey and Carlton E. Wilson, Spurring a Dialogue To Place the African European Experience Within the Context of an Afrocentric Philosophy, Journal of Black Studies, Vol. 25, No. 1, Sep. 1994.

Irish Republican Army symbolism; engaging the Red Hand as a possible reiteration and rendering of The Hand of Fatimah. Focusing on the Irish anti British occupation protest aesthetics, and practice, and engaging a scholarly study of British flag burning and immolated symbols. I appropriately titled my project, "Burning the Union Jack".

Years later; forming Amer African political ritual for Orun; burning confederate flags, "Old Dixie", was obviously appropriate. Following my established train of thought, it seemed a most efficient way to ritually decolonize minds in dynamic ceremony. I'm sure Orun are not the first to burn confederate flags. That being said, "The Lit Dixie", representing Orun covenant with the U.S. government, and sacrifices made for the future Orun State, is a unique act instituted and regularized ceremonially: preserved, and ritually practiced.

Orun Nation, Orun Intelligencia, Orun Party, Orun State, Star Logic, Amer-African State Craft, Orun Census Practice and African American Political Ritual are necessary responses to EuroAmerico colonial infra state Political Witchcraft among other devices. Thus We understand the celestial significance and revelatory terrestrial experience of Orun State and Amer African Statecraft in past, present and future realities.

As the Holy Qur'an says, in the first verse of Surah Muminun, "The Believers", verse 1,

$$\text{قَدْ أَفْلَحَ الْمُؤْمِنُونَ}$$

"Surely the Believers are already successful."

We Praise The Most High for making Us successful in this most worthy of endeavors.

Amin.

Chorum Avum :
Occidental Dawn Chorus

*

º93

^

+

&
Di
Vine Lullaby
Loblolly Chimes High
Science Prime Signs
Hematite Meteorites Burned
Cheeks   Diaboliques   Heartened
Gardens' Spirrigate Cry'n Carving
Artisans Most High Partisans Darkened
Courtesans Now Enlightened Clandestine
Destined
Regal Eagle
Natal
Cradle
Answered
Question
Led the
Heavens
Dawnward
Westward

---

93 Allegro, John Marco. *The Sacred Mushroom and the Cross: a Study of the Nature and Origins of Christianity Within the Fertility Cults of the Ancient Near East.* London: Hodder and Stoughton, 1970.

Harriet Follow Your Star [94]

---

[94] William Henry Johnson (March 18, 1901 – April 13, 1970) was an American painter. Born in Florence, South Carolina and is renowned for his "Primitavism".

Face of the Deep

Upon the Waters,
Spirit incubating
Generation...
     Rose Mountains,
Lifting Continents,
     From Oceans, Volcanos
...Puddling Great Lakes,
Letting there be Light, &
Birthing Our Babies...

Light Font ~ Star Bridge
Nafura Nawra : Buruj Miraj[95]

Asr Office Hours

Madonna in Kaaba

---

[95] *Nafura Nawra : Buruj Miraj* or "Fountain of Light : Stairway to Heaven" or "Light Font~Star Bridge"

⁹⁶Black Coffee Science⁹⁷
Framing Pan African Political Cosmology

ASA Brother Solomon,

Thank you again for sharing "Star Logic" and thank you for the note citation. First, thing that pricked my conscious mind and stood out was the art work and the esoteric symbolism that can and will be associated with how one interprets the book. The artistic and philosophical pieces truly compliment the journey and the cosmological, meta physical, and astrological interpretations possess and express the deep significance of the spiritual and political arrangements of the constellations. This literary interpretation allows

---

⁹⁶ Fahim A. Knight El, author of *In Defense of The Defender: a Critical Response to Attacks on The Honorable Elijah Mohammed* (1986); *Freemasonry (Moslem Sons) and Islam: What do They Share?*(2005); and the upcoming *Black Islam 360° Knowledge, Wisdom & Understanding,* (2021); *is the Chief Researcher for* the *KEEPING IT REAL* and *Arch-Hotep* Think Tanks. Baba Fahim is a Prince Hall Mason of Doric Masonic Lodge # 28 in Durham, NC and has been engaged in Masonic research for over 30 years.

⁹⁷ High Value conversations on the Supreme Wisdom, The Problem Book, and Actual Facts along with other NOI Lessons, historical, astronomical and metaphysical considerations, were called "Black Coffee Science" in the early Nation of Islam. El Hajj Malik Shabazz was the consummate "Black Coffee Scientist".

for Orun to be even further realized through "Star Logic".

Orun School leans into the tensions of how our experience in the United States, pre and post Civil War, created a social and political dichotomy, which impacted new cultural transformations. Acknowledging that rupture's roots and repair, on the *African* continent, as well as in the U.S., post-Chattel Slavery; is both, necessary and timely.

You've intentionally constructed the Orun Mandate to address nationhood, sovereignty and independence, with a new sense of directional urgency, beyond the traditional black power components. It distinctly moves away from a pure black nationalist ideological movement. I get that and there is no rebuttal from me. We are proud of you.

The grassroots "Nations", inside of the United States, will find much to identify with in STAR LOGIC and your *120-20 LESSONS* will captivate the attention of the various Black Masonic Islamic sects and movements. Simultaneously I believe the academic community will be intrigued by your insight, on introducing a different set of standards, regarding ADOS' ritual practices, with new sociological and psychological premises, interpretations, and decoded deceptive supremacist propaganda; whereby Corporate Military Elites have been playing chess, while ADOS, for lack of an informed intelligencia, have played checkers. Most will have no response; not because they do not desire to respond; because this is outside the box thinking and it is on another level.

-Baba Fahim A. Knight El
9/18/2020

Peace Brother Solomon,

"STAR LOGIC" is truly a living document. I initially appreciated the poetic artistic themes in the first initial drafts and the level of creativity without the philosophical commentary. It leaves the reader with a sense of mystique requiring imagination having deep roots in metaphysical, universal and cosmological realities, and covert sublime spaces, cemented by Higher esoteric principles (*The God(s?*) talking in the inner and outer universe). The *poetic* aspect of the work no doubt has the literary ability to stand on its own without the essays or explanation.

The infusion of the *Star Logic* essays, as Orun School thought, has brought a philosophical explanation, which some might not have obtained in the Poiesis; spurring a rethinking of how we historically and presently, carry out and perform our rituals, sacraments, rites, customs, and traditions. The chapter titled, "On Political Witch Craft" gives attention to this spiritual, sociological and psychological overstanding of the ritual practices adopted and adapted in the history of various aspects of our folklore as American Descendants of Slavery (ADOS).

The philosophical and programmatic approaches that you offer in "On ReNationalization" are refreshing. These approaches reflect strategies, tactics and devised approaches to engaging the various Orun "Nations", inside the United States, into various levels of constructive solidarity; being optimistic that with the right approach, we could establish the necessary covenants and planks of working toward organizational unity. Diffusing violence and anti-social behavior that has led to these various Nations and their social, political and counterproductive economic courses will be no easy task.

The chapter "Lit Dixie", showcases your literary ability and analytics; adding tremendous value with a glimpse into the your philosophical latitude, longitude, and intellectual range. This compliment is better justified and seen in the body of scholars that you assembled and relied on throughout the manuscript. The footnote citations once again are impeccable and academics should find them to be respectable and plausible and the detail given, should disallow any reason to dismiss the work as shoddy research.

The appendix, "Black Coffee Science: Framing Pan African Political Cosmology" substantiates and creates a different level of conversations, by addressing some of the ADOS specific considerations of geopolitics, statecraft, and sacred astronomy Thank you for your kindness and finding my words and critique of value and deciding to add them into your STAR LOGIC manuscript. I am humbled by this. All praises are due to Allah. Okay, who am I, I am just a grassroots brother that was trained by street enlighteners and I bucked on the other formal processes that were offered at my disposal. But this is my two cents. Keep it moving forward my Brother.

Baba Fahim A. Knight El
9/30/2020

Black Islam: 360°[98]
: Knowledge, Wisdom & Understanding :
"...Some Buttons..."[99]

---

[98] Fahim A. Knight El., *Black Islam: 360° :Knowledge, Wisdom & Understanding* : upcoming 2023   publication from Fahim and Associates with Lumifont Scriptorium

[99] **a.)** "...Some Buttons..." : Respective Seals of American Islamic Schools of Thought: Moorish Science Temple, Nation of Islam, Orun Nation, American Muslim Association; 5% Nation of Gods and Earths; compilation and ordering   by Fahim A. Knight El and Lumifont Scriptorium.

b.) *10. Why does Muhammad and any Muslim murder the devil? What is the Duty of each Muslim in regards to four devils? What Reward does a Muslim receive by presenting the four devils at one time?*

Answer: *Because he is One Hundred Percent wicked and will not keep and obey the Laws of Islam. His ways and actions are like a snake of the grafted type. So Muhammad learned that he could not reform the devils, so they had to be murdered. All Muslims will murder the devil because they know he is a snake and, also, if he be allowed to live, he would sting someone else. Each Muslim is required to bring four devils. And by bringing and presenting four at one time, his Reward is a button to wear on the lapel of his coat. Also, a free transportation in the Holy City (Mecca) to see Brother Muhammad* - Master Fard Muhammad, Supreme Wisdom, 1-14°, 10°, 1933, also 120° Lessons of Father Clarence 13X of the 5% Nation, 1967.

*Taking Devils' Heads is understood as subduing one's passions.

II. The Maurchives[100]
:Islam and Ancient Mystery Schools:
Professor Maurice L. Hines, July 1, 2018; Cairo

Is there a relationship between Islam and the mystery schools of the ancient world? This sounds like a strange comparison for someone who is only familiar with Freemasonry or for someone only familiar with the teachings of Islam. Yet, a close, open-minded reading of Freemasonic texts combined with a strong background in Islamic teachings and history will reveal a number of similarities between what is called the "Ancient Mysteries" and Islam as we know it.[101] I became

---

[100] a.) Professor Maurice Lee Hines of American University in Cairo, is an artist, activist, educator, Arabist, thinker, worshipper, community servant, and information specialist. His interests include African and African American History & Culture; Islamic History, Philosophy, Jurisprudence, Spirituality, Intellectual History; Arabic Language, Literature, Pedagogy ; Librarianship: Information Literacy, Archives, Classification of Knowledge; Black Consciousness, Afrocentricity, Pan-Africanism, Black Nationalism, Black Radicalism, Social Activism; Hip-Hop Culture & History in the U.S. & Africa; Egyptology, Ancient Mystery Schools & Religious Philosophies of the Ancient World Educational Philosophy in Islam, the West, and Ancient World. The Maurchives is an attempt to record some of his ideas around these topics and share them with the world. https://maurchives.com2018/07/01/islam-and-the-ancient-mysteries-part-1/ *additional footnote citations and commentary added by the Author for the edification of the Reader.

b.) Hines, Maurice, Interpretatio Islamica and the Unraveling of the Ancient Sabian Mystery, American University Cairo, 2023

[101] Fahim A. Knight-El; *Freemasonry (Moslem Sons) and Islam: What Do They Share?*, Fahim and Associates, Durham, N.C. 2005

aware of this relationship in my high school years when I read a book entitled, Stolen Legacy: Greek Philosophy is Stolen Egyptian Philosophy, by George G. M. James, originally published in 1954.[102] It stands as one of the pivotal works of African-centered studies of history. The author does not use the word Islam at all throughout the whole book, but he alludes to it in a section entitled, "How the African Continent gave its culture to the Western World," where he states:

During the Persian, Greek and Roman invasions, large numbers of Egyptians fled not only to the desert and mountain regions, but also to adjacent lands in Africa, Arabia and Asia Minor, where they lived, and secretly developed the teachings which belonged to their mystery system. In the 8th century A.D. the Moors, i.e., natives of Mauritania in North Africa, invaded Spain and took with them, the Egyptian culture which they had preserved. Knowledge in the ancient days was centralized i.e., it belonged to a common parent and system, i.e., the Wisdom Teaching or Mysteries of Egypt, which the Greeks used to call Sophia.

This passage prompted me to study Islam more seriously and to look at it from this historical perspective. Over the years, I would make mental notes of information I came across in the Islamic canon alluding to the idea of the Ancient Mysteries. However, before I can discuss the

---

[102] James, George G. M.. *Stolen Legacy: Greek Philosophy is Stolen Egyptian Philosophy.* London, United Kingdom, The African Publication Society, 1953.

Islamic sources and my interpretation of them, I must clarify exactly what the Ancient Mysteries are...

What were the Ancient Mysteries?

Also known as the Ancient Mystery Schools, this name is used by Freemasons, esotericists, and privy Afrocentrics to describe the catholic (i.e. universal) religion of the ancient world.[103] More specifically, it refers to the initiatic organization that taught and preserved religious teachings, the physical sciences, legislation, and the liberal arts among other things.[104] James gives a concise description of the Ancient Mystery Schools:

The ancient Egyptians had developed a very complex religious system, called the Mysteries, which was also the first system of salvation. As such, it regarded the human body as a prison house of the soul, which could be liberated from its bodily impediments, through the disciplines of the Arts and Sciences, and advanced from the level of a mortal to that of a God. This was the notion of the summum bonum or greatest good, to which all men must aspire, and it also became the basis of all ethical concepts.

---

[103] Guénon, René. The Crisis of the Modern World. United Kingdom: Luzac, 1946.

[104] Guenon, Rene. Perspectives on Initiation. United States: Sophia Perennis, 2004.

The Egyptian Mystery System was also a Secret Order, and membership was gained by initiation and a pledge to secrecy. The teaching was graded and delivered orally to the Neophyte; and under these circumstances of secrecy, the Egyptians developed secret systems of writing and teaching, and forbade their Initiates from writing what they had learnt. [105]

Given my description and James' statement above you might ask…How can a universal religion be secret?

First, it should be remembered that these schools were called "mysteries" because the primordial religion of mankind had no name by which it was referred. True adherents to the religion recognized it in others by their moral rectitude, erudition in the arts and sciences, as well as their keen knowledge of the narratives and symbols that were shared between all the religious orders of that time.[106]

Secondly, the notion of mystery and secrecy was used strategically. According to Albert Pike in his book, Morals and Dogma, secrecy was used to excite curiosity and to stir the emotions of those who might witness the passion plays of initiation. Likewise, they saw the spirit of mystery as coming

---

[105] James, George G. M.. Stolen Legacy: Greek Philosophy is Stolen Egyptian Philosophy. London, United Kingdom, The African Publication Society, 1953.

[106] Guenon, Rene. Perspectives on Initiation. United States: Sophia Perennis, 2004.

from God Himself, Who reveals Himself to the human heart in a manner that is unspoken.[107]

Furthermore, the true interpretations of the symbols, myths, and allegories were maintained by a scholarly/priest class who were not at liberty to share them with people who were not prepared to receive them. This took spiritual purity, which was only gained through the long and painful process of initiation. Only through this process, could other scholars and priests know that an initiate was prepared, strong, and trustworthy enough to uphold the doctrine, teach it accurately, and shield it and himself from corruption.[108]

The scholarly/priest class maintained chains of authorities and thus maintained the purity and accuracy of doctrines and practices. As James alludes to later in his book, it was the Greeks who learned from the Egyptians who broke this oath and consequently posited incomplete knowledge, which led to inaccuracies and misunderstandings of the original doctrines and practices.[109]

---

[107] Gen. Albert Pike, *Morals and Dogma of the Ancient and Accepted Scottish Rite of Freemasonry: Prepared for the Supreme Council of the Thirty-third Degree, for the Southern Jurisdiction of the United States, and Published by Its Authority.* United States: L. H. Jenkins, 1881.

[108] Guénon, René. Initiation and Spiritual Realization. United States: Sophia Perennis, 2001.

[109] James, George G. M.. Stolen Legacy: Greek Philosophy is Stolen Egyptian Philosophy. London, United Kingdom, The African Publication Society, 1953.

Mauristotle[110]
: CairO.G. :
MoOracle at Delphi.

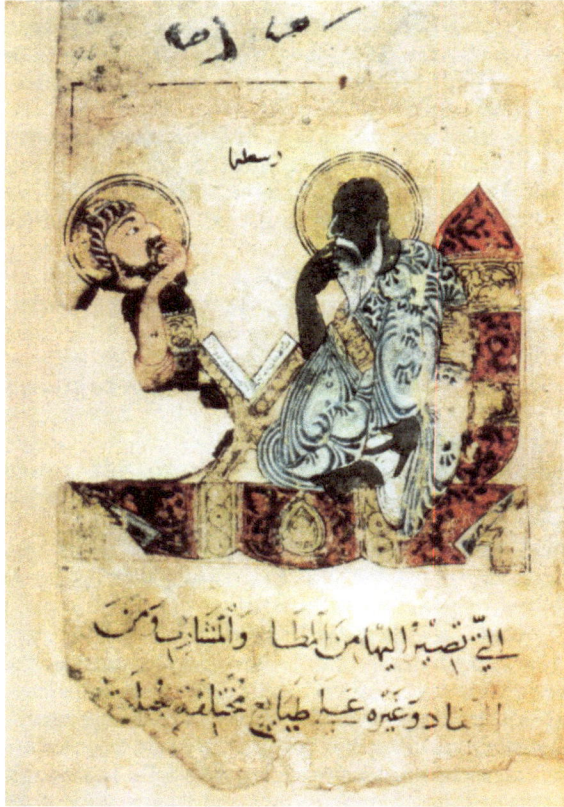

[110] **a.)** Professor Maurice Hines' is a Scholar*******General*******. See *Interpretatio Islamica and the Unraveling of the Ancient Sabian Mystery*, American University Cairo, 2023 .
b.) Illustration of Aristotle represented as a moor from 13th Century, Spain from Kitāb Naʿt al-Ḥayawān, "The World of Beasts". **c.)** Dr. George G. M. James asserts that Aristotle studied from texts that Alexander The Great Stole from the Royal Library in Alexandra.

The Maurchives
:*Rene Guenon vs. Modern Mystery*:
Professor Maurice Hines;
June 6, 2019; Cairo

I am convinced that no discussion of the Ancient Mystery Schools is complete without engaging the works of the French philosopher and purported founder of the Traditionalist school, Rene Guenon, also known as Abdul Wahid Yahya - Solayman Idris, 2002[111]

Rene Guenon grew up as a Catholic and later became immersed in the growing European occultist scene, joining the Freemasons, and what became known as the Theosophical Society. He was one of the major French commentators on metaphysics and the occult even though he did not complete his academic studies. He would later study a variety of Eastern religions like Taoism, Hinduism, folklore and other mystic traditions, writing extensively on them for European audiences.[112]

---

[111] While college roommates with Professor Hines; The Author was introduced to Rene Guenon, by Dr. Fuad S. Naim of, then Duke Islamic Studies, later of Georgetown Islamic Studies; while Idris and Naim worked together at the Regulator Bookshop in Durham, North Carolina.

[112] Waterfield, Robin. Rene Guenon and the Future of the West: The Life and Writings of a 20th Century Metaphysician. United States: Sophia Perennis, 2005.

Guenon came to oppose the European trends towards occultism, masonry, and theosophy, dismissing them as pseudo-religions and symptoms of a crisis in the modern European world. In doing so, he touches on a key point worthy of discussion. How was it that the ancient mysteries became associated with such trends?[113]

It was exactly these modern European groups that co-opted the notion of "the Ancient Mysteries," misconstrued the ideas of the Eastern spiritual paths, and attempted to separate

---

[113]**a.)** Guénon, René. Theosophy: History of a Pseudo-religion. United States: Sophia Perennis, 2004.**b.)** Claims to Solomonic lineage and Ancient Mystery bear Quranic commentary: Baqara 2:102

بِسْمِ اللهِ الرَّحْمَنِ الرَّحِيمِ

وَا مَا تَتْلُو الشَّيَاطِينُ عَلَىٰ مُلْكِ سُلَيْمَانَ وَمَا كَفَرَ سُلَيْمَانُ وَلَٰكِنَّ الشَّيَاطِينَ كَفَرُوا يُعَلِّمُونَ النَّاسَ السِّحْرَ وَمَا أُنْزِلَ عَلَى الْمَلَكَيْنِ بِبَابِلَ هَارُوتَ وَمَارُوتَ وَمَا يُعَلِّمَانِ مِنْ أَحَدٍ حَتَّىٰ يَقُولَا إِنَّمَا نَحْنُ فِتْنَةٌ فَلَا تَكْفُرْ ۖ فَيَتَعَلَّمُونَ مِنْهُمَا مَا يُفَرِّقُونَ بِهِ بَيْنَ الْمَرْءِ وَزَوْجِهِ وَمَا هُم بِضَارِّينَ بِهِ مِنْ أَحَدٍ إِلَّا بِإِذْنِ اللهِ وَيَتَعَلَّمُونَ مَا يَضُرُّهُمْ وَلَا يَنْفَعُهُمْ وَلَقَدْ عَلِمُوا لَمَنِ اشْتَرَاهُ مَا لَهُ فِي الْآخِرَةِ مِنْ خَلَاقٍ وَلَبِئْسَ مَا شَرَوْا بِهِ أَنْفُسَهُمْ لَوْ كَانُوا يَعْلَمُونَ

And they followed what the Shaitans (devils) chanted of sorcery in the reign of Sulaiman (Solomon), and Sulaiman (Solomon) was not an unbeliever, but the Shaitans (devils) disbelieved, they taught men sorcery and that was sent down to the two angels at Babel, Harut and Marut, yet these two taught no man until they had said, "Surely we are only a trial, therefore do not be a disbeliever." Even then men learned from these two, magic by which they might cause a separation between a man and his wife; and they cannot hurt with it any one except with Allah's permission, and they learned what harmed them and did not profit them, and certainly they know that he who bought it should have no share of good in the hereafter and evil was the price for which they sold their souls; had they but known this.

83

spirituality from religion. Guenon rightfully opposed these trends from the perspective of a European who had once been intimately intertwined with such groups and had come to study Eastern religions from their sources in the East. He was also privy to the intellectual fallacies and personal flaws of those in this movement, whose leaders were often charlatans.[114]

The Ancient Mystery Schools are not the same as the Modern Mystery Schools. The Ancient Mysteries, as we have elucidated before, was how humans maintained the revelations of the early prophets. In the Qur'an it is simply referred to as islam or the path of the Hanifs. Yet, Modern Mystery Schools tend to be hodgepodges of different religions or progenitors of supposedly new doctrines. Some of them lean towards mystical elements while others focus only on a material reality.[115]

The difference between true systems of spiritual knowledge and counterfeit systems is their ability to achieve a balance between the inner and the outer dimensions of human experience. Societies worldwide were based on the true systems, because their origins were from the Creator of human beings, its teachings maintained

---

[114]Guénon, René. The Spiritist Fallacy. United States: Sophia Perennis, 2003.

[115] Guénon, René. The Reign of Quantity and the Signs of the Times. United Kingdom: Luzac, 1953.

by the most knowledgeable and sincere in society. As such, they were wholistic enough for people to base their entire lives around them. In contrast, the counterfeit systems of modern times are responsible for the corruption of true systems of spiritual knowledge and the degeneration of societies, as they tend to promote the will of the individual over all things, devalue religious meritocracy by casting doubt on traditional institutions, and foster confusion and dissent among unsuspecting believers.

Though the Modern Mysteries had been gaining traction for a number of centuries prior, Rene Guenon was able to spot its influence at a critical junction in human history. In his book, *Theosophy: History of a Pseudo-Religion*, he tells of Helen Blavatsky's establishment of the Theosophical Society in the United States and her consequent introduction of a new international wave of occultism to the Western Hemisphere.[116]
In his critical biography of the life and works of Madame Blavatsky, Guenon establishes the archetype of the Modern Mystery leader. They often have a checkered history of crime and deception. Many American cult leaders followed in her footsteps, not the least of which have found

---

[116] Guénon, René. Le Théosophisme: Histoire d'une Pseudo-Religion. France: Éditions traditionnelles, 1965.

their way into African American communities[117], as noted by Wudjau Iry-Maat.[118]

Rene Guenon did a huge service by giving us a formula to unravel such cults by scrutinizing their biographies and exposing lies, inconsistencies, and destructive behavior. This allows us to limit the cult leader's sphere of influence among decent people. By understanding the ideological lineages and using clear logical language to deconstruct and challenge their philosophies. This allows for the long-term resistance to these organizations and their ilk.

Rene Guenon spent the last twenty years of his life in Cairo, Egypt, where he embraced Islam and joined the Shadhili sufi tariqa. According to various sources, he spent his time in spiritual reflection and publishing works that expounded on his ideas and combated the growing influence of the Modern Mystery Schools.[119]

---

[117] "Prophetic Masonic Islam", appended to The Sunrise in the West, Lumifont Scriptorium, 2019

[118]**a.)** Iry Maat, Wudjau Men-Ib. A Beginner's Introduction to Medew Netcher - the Ancient Egyptian Hieroglyphic System. United States: Heka Multimedia, 2015.**c.)** Aspects of Kwanza, Afrocentric Egyptologies, the "Conscious","Woke", "Black Girl Magic", movements can also be analyzed in this light.

[119] Chacornac, Paul. The Simple Life of René Guénon. United States: Sophia Perennis, 2005.

*

Weteor: "...a Lovely StarCoal Smudging..." [120]

[120] **a.)**   Michael D. Jones II of Durham, N. C. , is an author, illustrator, recording artist, educator, farmer, and humanitarian.http://clarioncontentmedia.com/2016/12/city-of-medicine-music-top-7-threat-assessment/

b.) Gen. 6:2-4 on meteorite worship as fertility cult and spiritual warfare:*2 That the sons of God saw the daughters of men that they were fair; and they took them wives of all which they chose. 3 And the Lord said, My spirit shall not always strive with man, for that he also is flesh: yet his days shall be an hundred and twenty years. 4 There were giants in the earth in those days; and also after that, when the sons of God came in unto the daughters of men, and they bare children to them, the same became mighty men which were of old, men of renown.*

3. *Above & Beyond Debate:*
Star Logic & Meteor Time
: Ancient Future Mystery I

My issue with AfroCentrism is that it hasn't gone Far Enough!!! - Dr. John Henrick Clark

Afrocentric paradigms are largely defined by Dr. George M. James' 1953 text *Stolen Legacy: Greek Philosophy is Stolen Egyptian Philosophy*[121]. *Stolen Legacy* told that most Greco-Roman philosophies were in fact African paradigms, gained by apprenticeship, and taken from The Library at Alexandria and other "Ancient Mystery Schools", during Europeans' conquests of Africa and the Middle East (also Africa[122]). This premise was understood as true enough by both Pre Socratic Greeks and 20th century revisionist Afrocentrists.

---

[121]**a.**) James, George G. M.. Stolen Legacy: Greek Philosophy is Stolen Egyptian Philosophy. London, United Kingdom, The African Publication Society, 1953.
b.) Dr. James taught Logic and Greek at Livingstone College, in Salisbury, North Carolina and earned his Phd from Columbia University in New York City.

[122] **a.**) The Middle East as a part of Africa separated by the Suez Canal for cultural colonization, Orun calls The Capture of Christ.
b.) Mazrui, A. (1992). Afrabia: Africa and the Arabs in the New World Order. Ufahamu: A Journal of African Studies, 20(3)

Among Others, Cheikh Anta Diop[123] and Martin Bernal[124] best credibly, and weightily substantiated many of *Stolen Legacy*'s claims in the 1970s through 2000s, with *The African Origin of Civilization: Myth or Reality, Precolonial Africa: A Comparative Study of the Political and Social Systems of Europe and Black Africa, from Antiquity to the Formation of Modern States,* and the *Black Athena: Volumes I-III.*

Stolen Legacy's premise, and Afrocentrism, in general, came under academic fire in the late 1990s. Interrogating *Stolen Legacy*'s source material; critical concerns were raised by Classics professors on methodological and epistemological grounds.[125] *Stolen Legacy*, Cheikh Anta Diop's works, and *Black Athena* were harshly impugned, by Professor Mary

---

[123] **a.**) Diop, Cheikh Anta., Cook, Mercer. The African Origin of Civilization: Myth Or Reality. United States: L. Hill, 1974

b.) Precolonial Black Africa: A Comparative Study of the Political and Social Systems of Europe and Black Africa, from Antiquity to the Formation of Modern States. Westport: L. Hill, 1987.

[124] **a.**) Bernal, Martin., Black Athena I: The Afroasiatic Roots of Classical Civilization: The Fabrication of Classical Civilization. United Kingdom: Free Association Books, 1987.**b.**) Black Athena II: The Archaeological and Documentary Evidence. United Kingdom: Rutgers University Press, 1991**c.**) Black Athena Writes Back: Martin Bernal Responds to His Critics. United Kingdom: Duke University Press, 2001.

d.) Black Athena III: The Linguistic Evidence; United States Rutgers University Press, 2008.

[125] Rogers, Guy MacLean., Black Athena Revisited. United Kingdom: University of North Carolina Press, 1996.

Lefkowitz in 1996's *Not out of Africa: How Afrocentrism Became an Excuse to Teach Myth as History.* While Diop's impeccably cited work was virtually unassailable, others were not. Emerita Lefkowitz exposed fabricated replicated notions of "Ancient Egyptian Mystery" in classical, renaissance, modern[126], Black and White, Masonic, narrative, histories, sourced by Afrocentrists , occultists and Others.

Lefkowitz's introduction to Afrocentrism was being called an implicit racist, by a black female graduate student, citing James, saying Socrates was Black, in a Greek philosophy course, at Wellesley College in 1991.[127] *Not Out of Africa* was her scholastic response. Schools of thought were further polarized along racial lines, as Lefkowitz attacked Black Classic Historians like Dubois and Frederick Douglas and Carter G. Woodson, for

---

[126] *Fabricated sourcing amongst historians and masons was first exposed in the 20th century by Rene Guenon in The Spiritist Fallacy (1923) and Theosophy: History of a Pseudo Religion (1928).

[127] **a.)** Lefkowitz, Mary., Professor Emerita of Classical Studies; Not out of Africa: How Afrocentrism Became an Excuse to Teach Myth as History. New York: Basic Books, 1996.**b.)** Rogers, Guy MacLean., Black Athena Revisited. United Kingdom: University of North Carolina Press, 1996.**c.)** Bernal, Martin., Black Athena Writes Back: Martin Bernal Responds to His Critics. United Kingdom: Duke University Press, 2001.

asserting that African Americans shared a lineage with Ancient Egyptians.[128]

---

[128]Bernal, Martin, Review of Lefkowitz, Not Out of Africa How Afrocentrism Became an Excuse to Teach Myth as History. Bryn Mawr Classical Rreview 1996.04.05 Review byMartin Bernal, Cornell University

Jacobs Eugenics[129] and Orun *Homo Sapiens Summa* Genomics[130] lays this argument to rest though, still her conversation with James over sources is interesting. Regarding fabrication of sources specifically: truths of James' and Lefkowitz's works were not accepted by either side. Orun School,

---

[129] Jacobs Eugenics: Brown Paper Bag Testing and American Population Management, appended to The Sunrise in the West, by Solayman Idris, 2019.

[130] **a.**)Solayman Idris, The Sunrise in the West, Lumifont Scriptorium for Nafura Nawra Buruj Miraj, Durham, N.C. 2019 *Who is Orun & What is Orun, are chapters in The Sunrise in the West, defining Orun as Homo Sapiens Summa, Complete Humanity, and the eventual culmination of the Human Genome.*
" ADOS and Orun differ in that ADOS are Orun before segregation and Orun is ADOS after desegregation and mingling and compiling the human genome. Shabazz, as in the "God Tribe" of the NOI, corresponds with Orun. Orun is Homo Sapiens Summa. Segregated society did not allow development into humanity's Prime Element."
"The "Divine Nation," Orun, are the primary ancestors and ultimate descendants of all humanity. ADOS, the current Orun Nation, also called Solar Orun, because slavery, success, and identity crises are mingled with all the nations of the world, recreating the complete genetic compilation of the originary Sun Tribe, who has until now been separated into different nations. Homo Sapiens Summa represents the proper speciation of Orun."
b.) Looking further into the characters of Orun and Orion, we might also note the Latin verb orior (rise, become visible) and its resonant constellation of cognates: origo (origin), oriens (east or orient, the direction of solar rising), and oriundus (about or needing to rise). - Dr. David Liu. Also, the Yoruba Orun, "Heavenly", correlates through the Arabic root a-r-n with the Persian Iran meaning "noble".

92

renders a necessarily synthetic perspective, in this regard.

Both James and Lefkowitz agree that Greek philosophy, *Out of Africa or Not*, survived the Medieval period through Moorish intellectuals. If ever legitimate Egyptian Mystery did exist in a European context; it would have at least possibly been carried, maintained, or accessed by the Africans occupying Spain, Portugal and Sicily from the 7th to 14th centuries.

It's generally accepted by scholars that the "Greek" Classics we have now are retranslated versions; back into Greek from meticulous Arabic copies; necessitated after the originals were ordered burned, by the Catholic Church.[131] Medieval Spanish representations of Socrates, Plato, and Aristotle; depict the Greek philosophical trinity as moors[132]; in scholarly muslim dress: in *jalabiyah*[133] often, with turbans on[134] This indicates that in

---

[131] Francis Newton, The Scriptorium and Library at Monte Cassino,1058-1105, Cambridge Studies in Palaeography and Codicology 7, Cambridge: Cambridge University Press, 1999.

[132] See CairOG : The Mauristotelian Discourse illustration, Star Logic (a collection of Poiesis) pg 91from A World of Beasts: A Thirteenth-century Illustrated Arabic Book on Animals (the Kitāb Na't Al-Ḥayawān) in the Ibn Bakhtīshū' Tradition, edited by Contadini, Anna. Netherlands: Brill, 2012.

[133] a traditional Arab garment worn by both males and females.

[134] Van Sertima, Ivan., The Golden Age of the Moor, Transaction Pub., 1991

medieval Europe, classical Greek philosophical works, were seen as, (translationally, if not epistemologically) derived from Afro Arabic sources, be they 'Greek' in original tongue, or not.[135] Neither Lefkowitz nor James spoke Arabic, so neither engaged Ancient Mystery understood as Andalusian Islamic Mysticism (Sufism(s)) properly.[136] Bernal's linguistic work in *Black Athena*, *Volume III*[137] fills some of this gap. Still, positive overlap in James' and Lefkowitz's works went unaddressed, in part because in addition to genuinely not liking the other side; neither school actively treated the Andalusian   assemblage of

---

[135] ibid

[136] a.) Hines, Maurice, Interpretatio Islamica and the Unraveling of the Ancient Sabian Mystery, American University Cairo, 2023

b.)The Maurchives: Islam and the Ancient Mystery Schools, I-IV and   Islam and the Ancient Egyptian Mystery Schools: The   Works   of   Dr.   Nadim al-Sayyar,   2018. Professor Hines' scholarly blog, The Maurchives,   introduces western   readers   to   primary   Arabic   sources   regarding Egyptian   Mystery   and   Islam, particularly the works of Dr. Nadim Sayyar. We anxiously await his upcoming Arabic and English language   publications   on theses and other topics. https://maurchives.com/2018/07/01/islam-and-the-ancient-mysteries-part-1/

[137] Bernal, Martin., Black Athena III: The Linguistic Evidence; United States Rutgers University Press, 2008.

classical sources, Egyptian Mystery, and Afro Quranic Metaphysics in European contexts[138].

Early on, I mistakenly understood *Stolen Legacy* as saying that the Greeks stole all important ideas and philosophies from the Egyptians, claiming them as their own. I had a whole image in my mind of white pirates stealing books from burning   Black libraries. This was perhaps a manufactured opinion.   In the least it was only a partial understanding of Dr. George G. M. James' complete thesis.

Bro. Hussein Fennel-Bey explained that ; though Dr. James posits that Alexander the Great, specifically stole scrolls from the Royal Library of Alexandria; not *all* Greek philosophical and metaphysical knowledge was *Stolen* from Africans. James acknowledged that many Greeks freely went to Egypt to learn, and were well taught there.   He says that the *Legacy*, the *credit* for the *origin* of the *wisdom (gnosis/knowledge)*; *the goal* of the philosophy; was *Stolen.*[139]*Stolen Gnosis,* does indeed, have a ring, to it.

---

138   a .) Hines, Maurice, Interpretatio Islamica and the Unraveling of the Ancient Sabian Mystery, American University Cairo,   2023

b.) On the Relationship between Islam and Mystery Schools, Parts I and II; interview conducted by the Author, at Melanintelligence, Nov. 19, Durham, North Carolina, 2018
https://www.youtube.com/watch?v=Xfl0j0N19-0&t=1744s
https://www.youtube.com/watch?v=KyalYGTrohY

139 Fennel Bey, Hussein., interview conducted by the Author at Melanintelligence, Durham, North Carolina, 2020

Martin Bernal adds in *Black Athena Volume I: The Fabrication of Classical Civilization,* that the African role in the genesis of western intellectual thought was eclipsed by later Greek nationalist sentiments and Greater Europe's need to rally against the Ottoman Turk Caliphate.[140] Still, Lefkowitz rigorously maintains insular 6th Century B.C. development of the Greek scholastic academic philosophical tradition; citing Ancient Mystery sycophancy as a source of Classical Greek scholarly claims of Egyptian genealogy of intelligence. Lefkowitz posited that some ancient Greeks proudly claimed that their cult(ure) was Egyptian in origin, not because it was true, but because it legitimized their authority to those who; much like today; fetishized Nile Valley Civilizations, without actually having been.[141] It was much riskier to travel to Egypt, for ancient Greeks, than it is for anyone now. It's an interesting thought.

Whether classical Greek claims to Egyptian heritage were true or not, Bernal says that later, Hellens, for political and ethnic reasons, began to assert insular origin of their cultural intelligences;

---

[140] Bernal, Martin., Black Athena I: The Afroasiatic Roots of Classical Civilization: The Fabrication of Classical Civilization. United Kingdom: Free Association Books, 1987.

[141] Lefkowitz, Mary., Professor Emerita of Classical Studies; Not out of Africa: How Afrocentrism Became an Excuse to Teach Myth as History. New York: Basic Books, 1996.

particularly their methodologies of scholastic and academic thinking; properly called "philosophy".[142]This was directly related to the Greek War for Independence, against the Ottoman Empire from1821-1832.[143] For Nationalist reasons, Greece was made European and her Mediterranean African Mother was exiled from modernity.

(Pre) Socratic, Platonic, and Aristotelian metaphysics have echoes from *The Ancient Egyptian Coffin Texts*[144]and *The Book of Coming Forth by Night*[145] also called *The Ancient Egyptian Book of the Dead*[146]. Still, according to Lefkowitz, The library at Alexandria was founded by Macedonian Greeks at least 30 years after Aristotle's death. This would mean that James' dates for the Alexandrian Royal Library looting, and sacral study by Aristotle of

---

[142] Bernal, Martin., Black Athena I: The Afroasiatic Roots of Classical Civilization: The Fabrication of Classical Civilization. United Kingdom: Free Association Books, 1987.

[143] ibid.

[144] The Ancient Egyptian Coffin Texts: Spells 788-1185 & indexes. United Kingdom: Aris & Phillips, 1973.

[145] Ashby, Muata. The Book of Coming Forth by Day. United States : Cruzian Mystic Books, 1998.

[146] The Egyptian Book of the Dead: The Most Ancient and the Most Important of the Extant Religious Texts of Ancient Egypt. United Kingdom: G.P. Putnam's Sons, 1894.

stolen scrolls from Ægypt were off.[147] It's a [not] small thing.

Frenchman turned AfroArabic Metaphysician, Shaykh Abdul Wahid Yahya a.k.a. Rene Guenon, asserted that the term "philosopher", meaning, "lover of wisdom", is primarily the designation of a student; denoting an inclination towards wisdom and a prerequisite condition for acquiring it[148]. Essentially, Guenon contends that being a philosopher does not mean that one has acquired wisdom or is wise. As to *philosophy*: Having love (*philo*) for a thing does not mean that you have acquired or created(*poiesis*) that thing (*Sophia*). Quite the opposite: It means one seeks that thing; that one is on a path. That is to say that claims to possession of *Stolen* student status; that of a philosopher, or philosophy, even be they classical; at a certain stage, can be understood as beneath Higher Intelligence.

For some of Us: Why Argue? For Others of Us: understandably, James, necessarily wrote one of the best works in the field; raising critical questions, leading to the illumination of white classical scholarly hubris, fabrication of sources, practice of pseudo mystery, and the *Theocide* of

---

[147]Lefkowitz, Mary., Professor Emerita of Classical Studies; Not out of Africa: How Afrocentrism Became an Excuse to Teach Myth as History. New York: Basic Books, 1996.

[148] Guénon, René. The Crisis of the Modern World. United Kingdom: Luzac, 1946.

modern European societies, who colonized their intellectual forefathers, and murdered their former gods.[149] This is in part what Orun calls *The Capture of Christ.*[150]

Melanintelligence constellates *Stolen Legacy* and *Not Out of Africa* with V.Y. Mudimbe's *On the Invention of Africa*[151] and *In the House of Lybia*[152]. Orun acknowledges Lefkowitz's exposure of dubious sources and reasserts *Stolen Legacy*'s thesis as *still* true. Mudimbe agrees with Lefkowitz that *philosophia* as a practice emerged from Athens in the late 5th Century. Mudimbe also agrees with James that the greater matrix of Mediterranean intelligence (which Mudimbe calls *gnosis*) furnished the foundational *materia* for *Sophia*. Hence, via *gnosis,* philosophy's origins, can be historically situated in Afrabian Matrix; Mudimbe calls Libya. Melantelligence understands Nubio-Lybian

---

[149] **a.)** Diop, Cheikh Anta. *Civilization Or Barbarism: An Authentic Anthropology.* United States: Chicago Review Press, Incorporated, 1988.
b.) Guénon, René. *Theosophy: History of a Pseudo-religion.* United States: Sophia Perennis, 2003.

[150] See Dusk Orientalis, Section 11 The Capture of Christ : Colonization as Theocide, 2020

[151] Mudimbe, Victor Yves., Mudimbé, Vumbi Yoka. *The Invention of Africa: Gnosis, Philosophy, and the Order of Knowledge (African Systems of Thought)* 1st Edition. United Kingdom: Indiana University Press, 1988.

[152] Mudimbe, V. Y.. The Mudimbe Reader: "In the House of Libya". United States: University of Virginia Press, 2016.

Meteoric Intelligence, called *Gnosis* (Knowledge) by Mudimbe, as the origin of *Sophia* (Wisdom), and thus, love of that wisdom; *philo Sophia*, was the search for what is now traditionally maintained in Afro-Arabic Qur'anic Metaphysics[153] called *Tasawuuf*, Sufism, and *Irfan*[154]; also called High Science & I.S.L.A.M,[155] Moorish Science[156]&

---

[153] Hines, Maurice.,On the Relationship between Islam and Mystery Schools, Parts I and II; interview conducted by the Author, at Melanintelligence, Nov. 19, Durham, North Carolina, 2018 https://www.youtube.com/watch?v=Xfl0j0N19-0&t=1744s
https://www.youtube.com/watch?v=KyalYGTrohY

[154] Ezzati, A.., 'Izzatī, Abū al-Faẕl. Islam and Natural Law. United Kingdom: ICAS Press, 2002.

[155] **a.) I S**elf **L**ord **A**m **M**aster (I.S.L.A.M.)- 120 Lessons, Supreme Alphabet, Clarence 13X, 1963
b.) Knight- El, Fahim A., Black Ilam 360°, Fahim and Associates, Durham, North Carolina 2021

[156] Ali,Timothy Drew., Najee-ullah El, Tauheedah S.. The Holy Koran of the Moorish Holy Temple of Science - Circle 7: Re-print of Original 1926 Publication. N.p.: Califa Media Publishing, 2020.

K.O.R.A.N.[157], and now *Star Logic*, by Orun, the Black Muslims and Moslem Sons.[158]

Professor Mudimbe reminds all Classicists that Ancient Greece was part of a economy of constant exchange with the greater Mediterranean, especially North Africa, then called "Libya", in Greek and the indigenous south Mediterranean tongue. For the ancients, racial groupings would be the last criteria by which they designated themselves in contrast to others, be they "African", "European", "Black" or "White": they are all more or less constructions of modernity and the colonial enterprise.[159]In debates as to what to call "Africa" from an afrocentrist decolonial perspective, alongside *Nubia[160]*; Mudimbe's recommendation of

---

[157] **a.**) **K**nowledge**O**rder**R**hythm**A**stronomy**N**ature (K.O.R.A.N.) - Bro C. Freeman El **b.**) Ali, Drew., Najee-ullah El, Tauheedah S.. The Holy Koran of the Moorish Holy Temple of Science Circle 7: Re-print of Original 1926 Publication. N.p.: Create Space Independent Pub, 2014.

[158] Foreword to Fahim Knight's Black Islam 360°: Knowledge Wisdom & Understanding written by Solayman Idris, 2021

[159] Mudimbe, Victor Yves., Mudimbé, Vumbi Yoka. The Invention of Africa: Gnosis, Philosophy, and the Order of Knowledge (African Systems of Thought) 1st Edition. United Kingdom: Indiana University Press, 1988.

[160] Precolonial Black Africa: A Comparative Study of the Political and Social Systems of Europe and Black Africa, from Antiquity to the Formation of Modern States. Westport: L. Hill, 1987.

"Libya" stands out as most appropriate[161]. Continuity of Mudimbe's AfroArabicLatino *Gnosis* was perhaps overshadowed because Lefkowitz nor James spoke Arabic to engage primary sources. Arabic is the language of modern Egypt and the most spoken language in Africa, and was the lingua franca of the medieval world[162]. James best told Orun what and where Egyptian Mystery is. Lefowitz does the same and says what it is not. Bernal intervenes with a genealogy of intelligence from at least Diodorus through Andalusian Moorish Science to medieval alchemy and possibly some renaissance hermeticists. *Black Athena: The Afro Asiatic Origin of Classical Civilization: Volume III, The Linguistic Evidence*, shows common etymologies between the language of Andalusian Arabic *AfroGnosis'* and the Phoenician rooted ritual

---

[161] **a.**) Mudimbe, V.Y., "In the House of Libya"   from The Mudimbe Reader. United States: University of Virginia Press, 2016.

b.) This reading came about from a conversation with Trip Attaway; Dr. Mudimbe's assistant from 2008-2014.

[162]   a.) Hines, Maurice, Interpretatio Islamica and the Unraveling of the Ancient Sabian Mystery, American University Cairo, 2023

b.) Hines, Maurice.,On the Relationship between Islam and Mystery Schools, Parts I and II; interview conducted by the Author, at Melanintelligence in Durham, North Carolina, on Nov. 19, 2018 https://www.youtube.com/watch?v=Xfl0j0N19-0&t=1744shttps:www.youtube.com/watch? v=KyalYGTrohY

[163]language of Delphi Oracle   Cult.[164]
Archeological work in Volume II resurrects the
Egyptian Mystery in Delphic History.   What is
actual *Mystery* though? What is it all for?

---

[163] a.) "An equally clear Semitic etymology is that
of βαιτνγοϛ(1CE) "sacred stone dropped from the
sky" from the Hebrew Bêt >e-l, Bethel "house
of God." Chantraine argues that the etymology
is "unknown." He sees it as a "Mediterranean"
religious term accepted in both Greek and Semitic
and that the notion of "house of God" was merely
a folk etymology."-Black Athena III: the Afro-
Asiatic Roots of Classical Civilization; The
Linguistic Evidence;   United States Rutger
    o   s   University   Press,   2008.
b.) See Also, Allegro, John Marco. The Sacred Mushroom
and the Cross: a Study of the Nature and Origins of
Christianity Within the Fertility Cults of the
Ancient Near East. London: Hodder and Stoughton, 1970.
c.) Guénon, René. Le Roi du Monde (The King of The World),
Chapter 9: The Omphalos and the Sacred Stones. France: Ch.
Bosse, 1927.

[164] Bernal, Martin., Bernal, Martin., Black Athena: the Afro-
Asiatic Roots of Classical Civilization; Volume II: The
Archeological Evidence

[165] a.)*Surah Rahman* [55:6](#) وَالنَّجْمُ وَالشَّجَرُ يَسْجُدَانِ

"...and the stars and the trees fall down"

b.)*...lest thou lift up thine eyes unto Heaven, and when thou seest the Sun, and the Moon, and the Stars, even all the Host of Heaven, shouldest be driven to worship Them, and serve them, which the LORD thy God hath divided unto All Nations under the Whole Heaven*-Deuteronomy 4:19, KJV London U.K., 1611

c.)*Properly, COELVMEMPIREVM HABITACVLVM DEI OMNIVM ELECTORVM, The Kingdom of Heaven, Dwelling place of God, and All the Elect.* - Ptolemy, *AlMagest*, 147 CE

NON NOBIS DOMINE SED NOMINI TUO DE GLORIAM-Not Ours Lord; To Your name All Glory- Psalms 113:9 Vulgate; 115:1 in Greek/Hebrew numbering; opening Mass.

*Jerry Lee Lewis, *"Great Balls of Fire"*, off *You Win Again,*1957

Star Logic & Meteor Time:
Ancient Future Mystery II

Melanintelligence' addition into the James - Lefkowitz debates engages Meteor Time, as Qur'anicly informed intuitive historiography[166]. Star Logic sees Stone Age meteoric tracking & impact excavation & extraction sciences, as the major operative spurs of advanced pre ancient societies; lending themselves to celestially born(e), terrestrially proliferated, Higher Intelligences.[167]

---

[166] **a.)** *Intuitive Historiography* designates narrative literatures, of pre ancient and classical civilizations, produced by secret societies of the late 19th and early 20th centuries.- Dr. Cheryl Spinner, University of Maryland, College Park; interview by author, at Duke University, Durham, N.C., 2017.
b.) Spinner, Cheryl, *Debunk Me Not: Magic and Marginalization, 1848 to the Present* (manuscript in progress), 2020
c.) Melanintelligence use of *Intuitive Historiography* differs from Dr. Spinner's coined   term to speak on and evaluate, specifically magical literature. Engaging Arabic metaphysics; In sufism and irfan; *seher* (sorcery) سحر magic and *seyer* (Divine Secrets) سِر, are clearly delineated in ways that they are not in Western phenomenology. Melanintelligence is not magic. We, Ourselves, are Divine Secrets.

[167] *Idris, Solayman, The Sunrise in the West, Section 6: "When is Orun"*

Sentient Meteoric Intelligences : the   Qur'anic
shihab[168] ,

---

[168] *al shihab, meteor,* الشِهَابُ

بسم الله الرّحمَن الرّحيمِ
وَلَقَدْ جَعَلْنَا فَي السَّمَاءِ بُرُوجًا وَزَيَّنَّاهَا لِلنَّاظِرِينَ
وَحَفِظْنَاهَا مِن كل شَيْطَانٍ رَّجيمٍ
إِلَّا مَنِ اسْتَرَقَ السَّمْعَ فَأَتْبَعَهُ شِهَابٌ مُبِينٌ

It is We Who have set out the zodiacal signs in the heavens, and made them
fair-seeming to (all) beholders;
And (moreover) We have guarded them from every cursed devil:
But any that gains a hearing by stealth, is pursued by a flaming fire, bright
(to see). -Surah Hijr, 15: 16-18

106

[169] **a.**) rujuma, meteor, projectile, ejected رُجُومًا ; also the r-j-m
رجم root gives us rajim meaning " (r)ejected" or "cast down"

عضو بالله منشطنر رجيم

"I seek refuge in Allah from shaytaan the rejected/cast down."
The juxtaposition between Raheem and Rajeem denoting,
angelic and diabolic, dispensation and fall; blessing and curses,
respectively, is worthy of note. An etymological entendre of the
name Lucifer in Latin is lux ("light") + fero ("bear, carry") also +
ferrum (iron) /ferro (sword) = meteorite. All symbols are subject
to multiplicity (if not inverse) interpretation. Guenon said
"Confusion of the light and dark and aspects of symbolism is the
essence of Satanism." Suffice to say the Orun in not luciferian,
satanic, or diabolic, or star worshipers. Avoiding
mischaracterization and following the advice to "Let not your
good be evil spoken of (Rom.14:16)". We give encompassing
commentary and take arrows from enemies' quivers. Returning
to the sublime; it should also be noted that the stars (najm) of
Surah Rahman, "The Compassionate", "fall" as in "prostrate"
(yasjudan), denoting willing submission, versus the (rajeem)
casting down and (r)ejection of the devils dismissed in the prayer
above and in Surahs Mulk and Hijr. The relationship of
between Raheem and rajeem representing sublime and infernal
possibilities, in every salat, is Spiritual Mystery and Ethical
Secret(s). Khalif Ali said in Nahjul Balagha that for the true
believer, paradise and hellfire present themselves every second,
every day.

b.)Surah Mulk
بسم الله الرحمن الرحيم
وَلَقَدْ زَيَّنَّا ٱلسَّمَآءَ ٱلدُّنْيَا بِمَصَٰبِيحَ وَجَعَلْنَٰهَا(5)
رُجُومًا لِّلشَّيَٰطِينِ ۖ وَأَعْتَدْنَا لَهُمْ عَذَابَ ٱلسَّعِيرِ

"We have adorned the lowest heaven with lamps and We have made them
[these lamps] a means of bombardment on the devils and have prepared for

and *hujarat*[170]; denote different modes of meteorite, representing angelic and diabolic elements.[171] The "Many Comets"[172] of the Seal of Orun, represent Orun Intelligencia, The Houses of Orun, Angelic Protection, Meteor Time, and the advent of The Orun Age (Orunage).[173]The ritual "stoning of the devil", in the Kaaba, on Hajj pilgrimage is

---

[170] a.) Surah *Al-Hujurat* (الحجرات) 49

b.) *al hujurat* in the Qur'an means "inner rooms" and in Arabic language also means "foundation stones" as well as "meteorites".

[171] *...It is a tesserated pavement, with an indented border round it. The pavement, alternately black and white, symbolizes, whether so intended or not, the Good and Evil Principles of the Egyptian and Persian creed. It is the warfare of Michael and Satan, of the Gods and Titans, of Balder and Lok; between light and shadow, which is darkness; Day and Night; Freedom and Despotism...-* General Albert Pike, Morals and Dogma, 1°, 1881
Pike, author of Morals and Dogma in 1871, created the liturgy and ritual of the KKK.- Dubois, Reconstruction, and the KKK: a Luminary Engagement with Shadow Organization (96th Annual ASALH Convention, themed, "African Americans and the Civil War", Richmond V.A., October, 2011) by Solomon Burnette citing Ku Klux Klan - Its Origin, Growth and Disbandment (1905), by Walter L. Flemming.

[172] a.) Star Logic recognizes astronomical differences between comets, meteors,, asteroids, and fulgurites (understood as atmospherically generated earth stones).   While all of these present phenomenally and sometimes materially different elements; symbolically comets, asteroids, meteors meteorites, and fulgurites,   have the concurrent symbolism representing communication between multiple states of being and spiritual and initiatic hierarchies.

[173] *The Sunrise in the West,* " Symbolic Lexicon: The Seal ofOrun", 2019

meteoric symbolics.   The Prophet's *Isra* and *Miraj*(ladder to heaven): His one Night's *Travel (isra)* and *Ascent(miraj)* , from Mecca to Jerusalem ,and up through the Seven Heavens on *Buraq: lightening*; will be treated specifically in Dusk Orientalis.[174]

In the formative sense, to a *meteorological* degree, the "Thunder Stones" of Yoruba lore[175]bear note. Angelic Meteorics are regularly engaged as weapons of spiritual warfare even today.   Orun School understands AfroQuranic

---

174 *Dusk Orientalis, 2021; *miraj and *rujum* have relationship
* *Isra*"The Journey"17:1, *Najm* The Star13-19 الإسراء والمعراج

[175] **a.**) Sangode, Ayobunmi Sosi. The Cult of Sango: The Study of Fire : an Anthology. United States: Athelia Henrietta Press, 1996.
b.) Guénon, René. Le Roi du Monde (The King of The World), Chapter 9: The Omphalos and the Sacred Stones. France: Ch. Bosse, 1927. **c.**) Meteorics, the study of asteroids, comets, and such, should not be confused with Meteorology, more commonly, the study of atmospheric dynamics. In this same way "Thunder Stones", or "Chango Stones", as fulgural glass made from lightening strikes; are insular earthly phenomena, manifest between firmament (literally in thunder storms) and earth. In contrast, Meteoric fulgural glass, such as Tutankhamen's yellow obsidian scarab charm: as manifest between star (literally outer space) and earth: is created by the impact of a meteorite.
d.)discussion of Cosmological correspondences of Ife divination, properly called Orunmilla, "Heaven's Salvation "   as possible representative meteoric technology;   included in   "Foundation Stones from the Heights", Dusk Orientalis: Times of the Signs III, 2021.

Meteorics as tools of manifest spiritual warfare[176]: necessary knowledges revealed for empowerment of ADOS; in addition to being the foundational

---

[176] **a.)** Surah Al Mulk

بسمِ اللهِ الرّحمَنِ الرّحيمِ

وَلَقَدْ زَيَّنَّا السَّمَاءَ الدُّنْيَا بِمَصَابِيحَ وَجَعَلْنَاهَا رُجُومًا (5) لِلشَّيَاطِينِ وَأَعْتَدْنَا لَهُمْ عَذَابَالسَّعِيرِ

"We have adorned the lowest heaven with lamps and We have made them [these lamps] a means of bombardment on the devils." (67:05)

b.) Surah Al Hijr

بسمِ اللهِ الرّحمَنِ الرّحيمِ

(6) وَأَنَّهُ كَانَ رِجَالٌ مِّنَ الْإِنسِ يَعُوذُونَ بِرِجَالٍ مِنَ الْجِنِّ فَزَادُوهُمْ رَهَقًا(7) وَأَنَّهُمْ ظَنُّوا كَمَا ظَنَنتُمْ أَن لَّن يَبْعَثَ اللهُ أَحَدًا(8) وَأَنَّا لَمَسْنَا السَّمَاءَ فَوَجَدْنَاهَا مُلِئَتْ حَرَسًا شَدِيدًا وَشُهُبًا(9) وَأَنَّا كُنَّا نَقْعُدُ مِنْهَامَقَاعِدَ لِلسَّمْعِ فَمَن يَسْتَمِعِ الْآنَ يَجِدْ لَهُ شِهَابًا رَّصَدًا

(6) 'And they (came to) think as ye thought, that Allah would not raise up any one (to Judgment). (7) 'And we pried into the secrets of heaven; but we found it filled with stern guards and flaming fires. (8) 'We used, indeed, to sit there in (hidden) stations, to (steal) a hearing; but any who listen now will find a flaming fire watching him in ambush. (9) 'And we understand not whether ill is intended to those on earth, or whether their Lord (really) intends to guide them to right conduct.

c.) *Surah Al Jinn*

بسمِ اللهِ الرّحمَنِ الرّحيمِ

وَلَقَدْ جَعَلْنَا فِي السَّمَاءِ بُرُوجًا وَزَيَّنَّاهَا لِلنَّاظِرِينَ (15) وَحَفِظْنَاهَا مِن كُلِّ شَيْطَانٍ رَّجِيمٍ(17) إِلَّا مَنِ اسْتَرَقَ (16) السَّمْعَ فَأَتْبَعَهُ شِهَابٌ مُبِينٌ

*It is We Who have set out the zodiacal signs in the heavens, and made them fair-seeming to (all) beholders; (16) And (moreover) We have guarded them from every cursed devil: (17) But any that gains a hearing by stealth, is pursued by a flaming fire, bright (to see).fire, bright (to see).**d.)** The cherubim's "flaming sword" of Genesis 3:24 guarding the Garden of Eden is understood as a meteorite in light of these Qur'anic commentaries.*

e.) *"...flaming swords; guarding Eden Torching Sodom..."- "Aerolith", Star Logic Collection, Lumifont Scriptorium, 2020*

intelligence of terrestrial civilization.[177] Star Logic Meteorics as legitimate Ancient Mystery, are a part of the pre Socratic economy of foundational mediating civilizational intelligences that George G. M. James termed *Stolen Legacies*. Subsequent civilizational sciences are latent products of meteoric engagement as Divine endeavor. The Qur'an, *Surah Al Hadid*, "The Iron", says "...and We *sent down* the iron, wherein is power mighty and benefits for the people..."[178]; scripturally

---

[177] **a.)** According to the Jafari School of Shia Islam, the Black Stone in the Kaaba called Hujurat al Aswad, is a petrified angel: a companion of Adam.- Sheikh Jafar Muhibullah, Interview conducted by the Author, titled, Al Farawis : The Riders of Hussein, post Majlis Lecture, at Madinah tul Ilm Center, Durham North Carolina, June, 2004

b.) Hon. Elijah Muhammad, in his "Theology of Time" lecture series (1972), said that he went to Mecca and kissed the black stone, though he was disappointed because he felt like he was making pilgrimage to himself.- Elijah Muhammad, The True History Of Elijah Muhammad: The Black Stone; (ed. Nasir Hakim), Secretarius Publications, 2008

[178] a.) *Surah al Hadid* 57:25 بِسْمِ اللهِ الرَّحْمَنِ الرَّحِيمِ

لَقَدْ أَرْسَلْنَا رُسُلَنَا بِالْبَيِّنَاتِ وَأَنزَلْنَا مَعَهُمُ الْكِتَابَ وَالْمِيزَانَ لِيَقُومَ النَّاسُ بِالْقِسْطِ وَأَنزَلْنَا الْحَدِيدَ فِيهِ بَأْسٌ شَدِيدٌ وَمَنَافِعُ لِلنَّاسِ وَلِيَعْلَمَ اللهُ مَن يَنصُرُهُ وَرُسُلَهُ بِالْغَيْبِ إِنَّ اللهَ قَوِيٌّ عَزِيزٌ

"Certainly We sent Our Messengers with clear proofs and We sent down with them the Scripture and the Balance that may establish the people with justice. And We sent down [the] iron, wherein (is) power mighty and benefits for the people, and so that Allah may make evident (he) who helps Him and His Messengers, unseen. Indeed, Allah (is) All-Strong All-Mighty."
b.) *Bronze Age Iron: Meteorite or Not; Chemical Strategy*; Journal of Archeological Science, Dec, 5 2017

111

referencing the meteoric origins of iron ore in the 7th Century.

The diabolical "cast down", "fallen stars", of the Book of Revelation[179] differ from the stars who *willingly* "made obeisance or prostrated" i.e. "fell down on their face" submissively before Joseph, representing different tribes' and nations' submission to the Most High.[180]

Erecting meteoric pillars like the Black Stone in the Kaaba is the Divine Standard for Ancient Near East Nation Building[181]. "Star Piling" was done by Abraham and Ishmael, constructing the

---

[179] *And his tail drew the third part of the stars of heaven, and did cast them to the earth: and the dragon stood before the woman which was ready to be delivered, for to devour her child as soon as it was born.* - Revelation 12:4

[180] *"... the sun and the moon and the eleven stars made obeisance to me. 10And he told it to his father, and to his brethren: and his father rebuked him, and said unto him, What is this dream that thou hast dreamed? Shall I and thy mother and thy brethren indeed come to bow down ourselves to thee to the earth? 11And his brethren envied him; but his father observed the saying."*-Gen.37:10 KJV

[181] **a.)** According to the Jafari School of Shia Islam, the Black Stone in the Kaaba called Hujurat al Aswad, is a petrified angel: a companion of Adam.- Sheikh Jafar Muhibullah, Interview conducted by the Author, titled, Al Farawis : The Riders of Hussein, post Majlis Lecture, at Madinah tul Ilm Center, Durham North Carolina, June, 2004
b.) Hon. Elijah Muhammad, in his "Theology of Time" lecture series (1972), said that he went to Mecca and kissed the black stone, though he was disappointed because he felt like he was making pilgrimage to himself.- Elijah Muhammad, *The True History Of Elijah Muhammad: The Black Stone*; (ed. Nasir Hakim), Secretarius Publications, 2008

Kaaba[182]; by Jacob (then Israel) at Bethel[183]twice; then again by Muhammad at the confederation of Mecca[184]; demonstrating continuation of primordial angelic meteoric pilgrimage migration cult.[185] The Black Stone in the Kaaba is said to

[182] Ibn al Kalbi., *Book of Idols*. Translated by Nabih A. Faris, of the American University at Beirut, United States: Princeton University Press, 1950.

[183] *"...And he dreamed, and behold a ladder set up on the earth, and the top of it reached to heaven: and behold the angels of God ascending and descending on it. 13And, behold, the LORD stood above it...And he was afraid, and said, How dreadful is this place! this is none other but the house of God, and this is the gate of heaven.*
18And Jacob rose up early in the morning, and took the stone that he had put for his pillows, and set it up for a pillar, and poured oil upon the top of it...[saying]And this stone, which I have set for a pillar, shall be God's house: and of all that thou shalt give me I will surely give the tenth unto thee.

[184] W. Montgomery Watt, *Muhammad at Mecca*, Oxford University Press, 1953. Chapter 4, *"The Unifying of the Arabs."*

[185] Deuteronomy 32:15 *But Jeshurun waxed fat, and kicked: thou art waxen fat, thou art grown thick, thou art covered with fatness; then he forsook God which made him, and lightly esteemed the Rock of his salvation.*

have been an angelic companion of Adam.[186] While "fallen star" is a common diabolic metaphor, every meteorite is not one of "The Fallen", per say. Angels sent on missions need be differentiated from genies cast down. The Heavens, in general, are richer, than what They have *thrown away...*

In part, what has lately passed as Egyptian Mystery til now, as Lefkowitz showed, was charlatan pageantry based on dubious sources.[187] Demonstrated "signs and wonders" of "modern mystery" is actually not ancient mystery; so much as *Secret Doctrine*[188]; rooted in magical study, seance, Theosophical and neo spiritualist practice in the 16th-18th centuries, by corporate military elite

---

[186] **a.)** According to the Jafari School of Shia Islam, the Black Stone in the Kaaba called Hujurat al Aswad, is a petrified angel: a companion of Adam.- Sheikh Jafar Muhibullah, Interview conducted by the Author, titled, *Al Farawis : The Riders of Hussein,* post Majlis Lecture, at Madinah tul Ilm Center, Durham North Carolina, June, 2004

b.) Hon. Elijah Muhammad, in his "Theology of Time" lecture series (1972), said that he went to Mecca and kissed the black stone, though he was disappointed because he felt like he was making pilgrimage to himself.- Elijah Muhammad, *The True History Of Elijah Muhammad: The Black Stone*; (ed. Nasir Hakim), Secretarius Publications, 2008

[187] Lefkowitz, Mary., Professor Emerita of Classical Studies; *Not out of Africa: How Afrocentrism Became an Excuse to Teach Myth as History.* New York: Basic Books, 1996.

[188] Guénon, René. *Theosophy: History of a Pseudo-Religion.* United States: Sophia Perennis, 2004.

(CME) occultists, whose spirit possession ceremonies yielded their "primary sources" on Ancient Mystery.[189] Alternatively, pseudo-mystery is rudimentarily gleaned from later dynastic hieroglyphic sources; constituting relatively new *Ancient* civilizational knowledges, rather than Celestine intelligence[190], coming from the Sidereal age of Orun, called the *Theoscene.[191]* Colonialist Occultist archaeologists imitated the illustrated forms from hieroglyphs and created denatured formulae and false doctrines to "activate" them as "Egyptian Mystery". This is grave robbing and political cannibalism on another level.

Star Logic orders Sidereal Orun Age, as Contained and Dispensed, potential and active, pregnant and birthed; Meteor Time. Sidereal Meteor Time is Pre ancient Eras measured by stellar bodies outside

---

[189] Guénon, René. *The Spiritist Fallacy.* United States: Sophia Perennis, 2003.

[190] Guénon, René. *The Reign of Quantity and the Signs of the Times.* United Kingdom: Penguin Books, 1972.

[191] "The Age of God" from "When is Orun", *The Sunrise in the West*, Lumifont Scriptorium, 2019

of our Solar System; in concert with meteor showers; spurring civilizational leaps.[192]

Engaging Dispensed and Contained meteor time, as Era markers; Star Logic uses sidereal elements to better measure, within and without, different Ages, increasing the scope of Melanintelligence astronomically, beyond that of modern historiography. Furthermore, by telling time by succession of meteor showers; with the sun, moon, stars and planets; Star Logic, redefines time and space, refocusing Orun on It's mobile

---

[192]**a.)** *...Egyptians may have the oldest documented civilization, the ancient Egyptians referenced Older, more advanced civilizations to themselves. What the ancients reference before them is The Age of Orun, called Sidereal Orun and Meteor Time. Our pre-ancient society was the Originary Sun Tribe. Sidereal Orun/ Meteor Time occurs both within and without Solar and Lunar time and space... According to Star Logic, both Orun Nation and Orun State's inception and birth, succeed one another, as Orun Meteor time initiates the Later Solar Orun Age. The Leonid Meteor Shower of 1833, marks the coming of the Orun Nation while the revolutionary founding of Orun State: latter Solar Orun Age, coincides with the arming and self defense of Orun Soldiers in 1863, during the American Civil War...* Orun Nation is Founded under the Leonid Meteor Shower of 1833; The year 2020 A.D. is the Solar Orun year 187-188, according to Meteor Time.

b.) ٱلرَّحْمَٰنِ ٱلرَّحِيمِ *Al Rahman and Al Raheem,* coming from the r-h-m ر - ح - م Arabic root literally meaning "womb" usually translated Gracious and Merciful respectively mean "the Container of Mercy," and "the Dispenser of Mercy." - Imam W. Deen Mohammed, The Meaning of Ar-Rahman [Lecture], Yusuf Shah Masjid, December 15, 2001."

c.) In essence, Time & Space are pregnant with Orun until birthed in Meteoric Intelligence.

116

histories and Celestine origins, activating epigenetic ancestral intelligences.[193]

Developing, Stone and Bronze Age societies, drew iron from mineral deposits in meteorites.[194] Most meteorites used in weaponry were iron nickel alloys.[195] Movement from Stone to Bronze Age and from Bronze to Iron Age[196] is in part due to

---

[193] a.) "On Renationalization", Star Logic Collection, 2020
b) Hortense Spillers', "Women and Republican Formation"; workshop organized by Franklin Humanities Institute; September, 2010, at Duke University with her commentary on the metaphysical language of the Haytian constitution of 1805 was generative in "Quranic Poetics of Black Republicans".
b.) Gumbs, Alexis Pauline. Spill: Scenes of Black Feminist Fugitivity. United Kingdom: Duke University Press, 2016.

[194] Saarinen, Oiva W.. From Meteorite Impact to Constellation City: A Historical Geography of Greater Sudbury. Canada: Wilfrid Laurier University Press, 2013.

[195] ibid

[196]Jarmon, Albert.,"Bronze Age Iron: Meteorite or Not;Chemical Strategy; Journal of Archeological Science, Dec. 5, 2017

contact with meteoric Celestine intelligences.[197] King Tutankhamen was buried with both a spear and an amulet; both made from meteoric elements.[198]   While The Boy King was interred with tons of gold and jewels; during his (life) time, the meteorite iron spear tip, and impact site yellow obsidian scarab amulet, were worth more than the fortune of his tomb.[199]

Deracinating Orun from our homeland; Corporate Military Elites (CMEs), demonized our language(s), submerged our bloodlines in the middle passage, Chattel tortured our ancestors, and Brown Paper bagged leadership; holistically rupturing Orun's very existence; creating a

---

[197] Dawud & Dhul Karnain's Qur'anic metallurgies are of note.

وَلَقَدْ آتَيْنَا دَاوُودَ مِنَّا فَضْلًا يَا جِبَالُ أَوِّبِي مَعَهُ وَالطَّيْرَ وَأَلَنَّا لَهُ الْحَدِيدَ

أَنِ اعْمَلْ سَابِغَاتٍ وَقَدِّرْ فِي السَّرْدِ وَاعْمَلُوا صَالِحًا إِنِّي بِمَا تَعْمَلُونَ بَصِيرٌ

Saba 34:10 *We bestowed Grace aforetime on David from ourselves: "O ye Mountains! Sing ye back the Praises of Allah with him! and ye birds (also)! And We made the iron soft for him;*

34:11 *(Commanding), "Make thou coats of mail, balancing well the rings of chain armour, and work ye righteousness; for be sure I see (clearly) all that ye do."*

آتُونِي زُبَرَ الْحَدِيدِ حَتَّى إِذَا سَاوَى بَيْنَ الصَّدَفَيْنِ قَالَ انفُخُوا
حَتَّى إِذَا جَعَلَهُ نَارًا قَالَ آتُونِي أُفْرِغْ عَلَيْهِ قِطْرًا

Al Khaf 18:96. *Give me pieces of iron - till, when he had levelled up (the gap) between the cliffs, he said: Blow! - till, when he had made it a fire, he said: Bring me molten copper to pour thereon.*

[198] Larsen, Jon. *In Search of Stardust: Amazing Micrometeorites and Their Terrestrial Imposters.* United States: Voyageur Press, 2017.

[199] a.)ibid b.) Oliver Farrington, "The Worship and Folk-Lore of Meteorites," Journal of American Folklore, 12/664, 1900, p. 200.

seemingly irrevocably anchored mental, time-space, inter generational spiritual colonization.[200] As to the transatlantic replacement of Orun religion: slavery stole *The Souls of Black Folk*.[201] Most of what devils didn't steal, sellouts sold. Star Logic directly addresses cultural eclipses and ruptures; (re)creating alternative time-space paradigms, allowing a break with the Gregorian calendar; that was imposed over, Orun's Afro Arabic Islamic lunar calendar, with the slave trade in 1555.[202]

Advancing societies first overtook others based on Iron Age technologies, weapons and axles, taken from meteorites.[203] Having mastered the science of charting and directing the movement and fall of meteorites; whenever one fell on a place or people, other than Orun, a team of

---

[200] *The Sunrise in the West; Why is Orun?*, 2019

[201] Du Bois, William Edward Burghardt. *The Souls of Black Folk: Essays and Sketches.* United States: A.C. McClurg & Company, 1903.

[202]see "On Political Witchcraft: Corporate Military Elite Sorcery as Black Population Management" from Star Logic (a collection of Poiesis) Lumifont Scriptorium, 2020

[203]Historical Metallurgy. United Kingdom: Historical Metallurgy Society, 1985 and J. A. Charles and A. L. Greer's
 Light Blue Materials: a History The Department of Materials Science And Metallurgy of Cambridge University, 1991

Star Logicians was sent out to retrieve it.[204] Upon contact, if a 'primitive' people inhabited around the impact site, the Star Logicians, then taught the 'primitives' to move, cut, extract elements out of, and venerate[205]the *Aerolith* or "sky stone", like at Delphi. Also called, *Lapis Exilis,* "meteorite" *"fine stone"* and in symbolism of building, *Lapsit Exilis* meaning "foundation stone" or "exiled stone".[206]. The concurrent speculation and operation of meteoric travel and foundation stones between the *Lapsit Exilis* at Delphi and the *Hujurat Aswad* (the Black Stone) in Mecca further cements this notion.

All subsequent civilizational sciences derive from Orun meteoric *modus operandi* **and** genealogy

---

[204] **a.**) Zavgorodniy Yu. Sacral Geography of Islam in the Works of Rene Guenon // Tradition and Traditionalism. Almanac (2014-2015). - Vinnytsia: Nilan, 2015. - P. 7-17.
b.) John Haywood;   Historical Atlas of the Ancient World 4,000,000 - 500 BC, Penguin Press, London, U.K.;   February 1, 2000

[205] Oliver Farrington, The Worship and Folk-Lore of Meteorites, Journal of American Folklore, Dec., 1900

[206]   **a.**) Guenon, Rene, Lapsit Exillis ,"Symbols of Sacred Science, Sophia Perennis Press,1962 and Psalm 18:22 with Matt. 21:42 refers to Lapsit Exilis as a name for the Holy
b.) Le Roi du Monde (The King of The World), Chapter 9: The Omphalos and the Sacred Stones. France: Ch. Bosse, 1927.
c.) Author interview with Duke University Classics' Department Pofessor Emeritus, Francis Newton, Durham, NC, 2020

of intelligence.[207] Star Logic and Meteor Time; the measurement and manipulation of meteoric energies, is the present, ancient, and future mystery; as it were.[208] The Greeks called their sacred meteorite, *Omphalos* or "navel". The Oracle at Delphi maintained the *Omphalos*. Meteoritic Delphic Oracular practice demonstrates Egypto Nubio-Lybian roots of the ancient Greek cult(ure).[209] The *Omphalos* Oracle cult is understood as a product of [meteoric] intelligence , *Gnosis* , exchange between Ancient Nubio-Lybians (Africans) and Greeks.

In tracing Gnosis' origins from NubioLibya, it's easier to prove Nile Valley and Delta origins of Delphi Oracle meteor cult relatively in 1000BC than it is to prove Athenian philosophical paradigm thievery in 600. Molefi K. Asante reminds us not to let white supremacist historicists

---

[207] "…Germination includes the hatching of a meteor, and the tap of a swallow's bill, breaking the egg; and it leads forward the birth…"-ALBERT PIKE, Morals and Dogma of the Ancient and Accepted Scottish Rite of Freemasonry ,prepared for the Supreme Council of the Thirty Third Degree for the Southern Jurisdiction of the United States: Charleston,1871.2°-Fellow-craft

[208]**a.)** Vagn F. Buchwald., Handbook of Iron Meteorites: Their History, Distribution, Composition and Structure, Volumes 1-3; Arizona State University. Center for Meteorite Studies; University of California Press, 1975

[209] Bernal, Martin., Black Athena: the Afro-Asiatic Roots of Classical Civilization; Volume II: The Archeological Evidence

decapitate Nubia from Egypt.[210]That being said, tracing the Nubio Lybian Delphi oracle cult actually makes the later exercise of challenging philosophy's origins unnecessary.Hip Hop Ambassador to the United Nations, KRS-One said "Its OK, to say that Egyptians invented writing and that Greeks invented books."[211]

---

[210] Molefi Kete Asante offers a synthetic perspective in *Egypt Vs. Greece and the American Academy.* United States: African American Images, 2002.

[211]a.) *"MCs Act Like They Don't Know"; KRS-One,* Elektra Records,1995 b.) Professor "Kr**I**s", **K**nowledge **R**eigning **S**upreme, Lawrence (KRS-One); Af Am Dept., Harvard University; Hip Hop Ambassador to the United Nations : Lecture Moogfest, The Carolina Theatre, Durham, North Carolina, May 19, 2018.

Orun gave the Delphiniums, Sidereal Ancient Mystery: meteoric measure & quarantine, excavation & transport, cutting[212] & extraction,

---

[212]a.)Blakely, Sandra. Myth, ritual, and metallurgy in ancient Greece and recent Africa. United Kingdom: Cambridge University Press, 2006. **b.**) Orun School recognizes The Rough Hewn and Perfect Hewn Ashlars of 1°Apprenticeship, as reference to the primitive state before and after contact with meteoric intelligence.- Gen. Albert Pike, *Morals and Dogma of the Ancient and Accepted Scottish Rite of Freemasonry: Prepared for the Supreme Council of the Thirty-third Degree, for the Southern Jurisdiction of the United States, and Published by Its Authority.* United States: L. H. Jenkins, 1881.***c.***) General Albert Pike[the quintessential corporate military elite CME*]; Grand Master of the Scottish Rite for the southern jurisdiction of the United States (whose headquarters were then in Charleston), was also in touch with Blavatsky around that time. But these relations seem to have had no sequel. It would seem in this case that Pike was more clear sighted than many others, and that he quite quickly recognized with whom he was dealing. Since we have the opportunity to do so so let us add that Albert Pike's reputation as a Masonic writer was quite overrated: a considerable part of his major work Morals and Dogma of Freemasonry is clearly plaigerized from Dogme et Rituel de la Haute Magie [*Dogma and Ritual of High Magic*]by the French occultist Eliphas Levi .[*Elephis Levi is most recognizable today for his rendering of the sabbatic goat, called "baphomet', used as a seal of the Church of Satan. In light of these considerations, perhaps Lefkowitz's attention would have been better turned towards Gen. Pike; rather that Dr. James*]- Guénon, René. Le Théosophisme: Histoire d'une Pseudo Religion. France: Valois, 1928. (Theosophy History of a Pseudo Religion) d.) Guenon said "…these relations *seem* to have had no sequel…" See "On Political Witchcraft: Corporate Military Elite Sorcery as Black Population Management", in this work, and "Prophetic Masonic Islam" from *The Sunrise in the West*, 2019 for further discussion.*comments in bracket are my own*

veneration & divination, science & technologies; leaving them with the Oracle Meteor Cult, to inform later epic Greek civilization.

The Oracle at Delphi then sent the Greek demigod heroes on (symbolic?) quests back to Africa to find their parents and "get made"; representing greater Greek society's quest for civilization.[213] This was seed enough, for Greeks to flourish, as travelers, seekers and lovers of wisdom : the *rest* of the "Philosopher's Stone(s)".[214]

Black Athena Volumes I & II: The Fabrication of Classical Civilization & The Archaeological and Documentary Evidence[215]go the distance proving the DelphiMeteora cult's extra Greco origins. Orun Intuitive Historiography; clarifies the hows and whys; the ways and means; "Myths" *and* "Realities"; of "The African Origin of Civilization".[216] Qur'anic study, Orun meteorics, and fugitive intelligence, as Star Logic bring

---

[213] THE SACRIFICIAL RITUALS OF GREEK HERO-CULTS IN THE ARCHAIC TO THE EARLY HELLENISTIC PERIOD by Gunnel Ekroth, University de Liege Press, 2002.

[214] Le Roi du Monde (The King of The World), Chapter 9: The Omphalos and the Sacred Stones. France: Ch. Bosse, 1927.

[215] Black Athena Volumes I & II: The Fabrication of Classical Civilization & The Archaeological and Documentary Evidence; Rutgers University Press, 1987; Duke University Press: United Kingdom,1991

[216] Diop, Cheikh Anta., Cook, Mercer. The African Origin of Civilization: Myth Or Reality. United States: L. Hill, 1974

Ancient Mystery [217]; within ADOS' grasp again, today. [218]   Corrupted ancient mystery led to the

---

[217]a.) Hines, Maurice, Interpretatio Islamica and the Unraveling of the Ancient Sabian Mystery, American University Cairo, 2023

b.)Hines, Maurice.,On the Relationship between Islam and Mystery Schools, Parts I and II appended; interview conducted by the Author, at Melanintelligence, Nov. 19, Durham, North Carolina, 2018 accessible on youtube here *https://www.youtube.com/watch?v=Xfl0j0N19-0&t=1744s*
https://www.youtube.com/watch?v=KyalYGTrohY

[218] Furthermore, it is said of the meteoric Black Stone in the Kaaba at Mecca : "It is called 'The Right Hand of God on Earth,'" Oliver Farrington, "The Worship and Folk-Lore of Meteorites," Journal of American Folklore, 12/664, 1900, p. 200.

degeneration of early societies[219] as well as ours.[220]

May the Most High protect us from the knowledge that is not beneficial.[221]Star Logic Meteoric Calendars with Sidereal span; along with cited BiblioQur'anic formulae, address and

---

219

بِسْمِ اللهِ الرَّحْمَنِ الرَّحِيمِ

وا مَا تَتْلُو الشَّيَاطِينُ عَلَىٰ مُلْكِ سُلَيْمَانَ وَمَا كَفَرَ سُلَيْمَانُ وَلَٰكِنَّ الشَّيَاطِينَ كَفَرُوا يُعَلِّمُونَ النَّاسَ السِّحْرَ وَمَا أُنزِلَ عَلَى الْمَلَكَيْنِ بِبَابِلَ هَارُوتَ وَمَارُوتَ وَمَا يُعَلِّمَانِ مِنْ أَحَدٍ حَتَّىٰ يَقُولَا إِنَّمَا نَحْنُ فِتْنَةٌ فَلَا تَكْفُرْ فَيَتَعَلَّمُونَ مِنْهُمَا مَا يُفَرِّقُونَ بِهِ بَيْنَ الْمَرْءِ وَزَوْجِهِ وَمَا هُم بِضَارِّينَ بِهِ مِنْ أَحَدٍ إِلَّا بِإِذْنِ اللهِ وَيَتَعَلَّمُونَ مَا يَضُرُّهُمْ وَلَا يَنفَعُهُمْ وَلَقَدْ عَلِمُوا لَمَنِ اشْتَرَاهُ مَا لَهُ فِي الْآخِرَةِ مِنْ خَلَاقٍ وَلَبِئْسَ مَا شَرَوْا بِهِ أَنفُسَهُمْ لَوْ كَانُوا يَعْلَمُونَ

And they followed what the Shaitans (devils) chanted of sorcery in the reign of Sulaiman (Solomon), and Sulaiman (Solomon) was not an unbeliever, but the Shaitans (devils) disbelieved, they taught men sorcery and that was sent down to the two angels at Babel, Harut and Marut, yet these two taught no man until they had said, "Surely we are only a trial, therefore do not be a disbeliever." Even then men learned from these two, magic by which they might cause a separation between a man and his wife; and they cannot hurt with it any one except with Allah's permission, and they learned what harmed them and did not profit them, and certainly they know that he who bought it should have no share of good in the hereafter and evil was the price for which they sold their souls; had they but known this.

220Guénon, René. *The Reign of Quantity and the Signs of the Times.* United Kingdom: Luzac, 1953.

221

اللّهُمَّ إِنّي أَعوذُ بِك مِن عِلم لا يَنفع ومِن قلب لا يَخشع ومِن نَفس لا تَشبع ومِن دُعاء لا يُسمع

O Allah, I seek refuge with You from knowledge that does not benefit, from a heart that is not humbly submissive; from a soul that is never satisfied, and from a supplication that is not given a response.

dislodge colonially time-space anchored political witchcrafts and portent the advent of Independent Orun Intelligencia.[222]

As the Holy Qur'an says,

قَدْ أَفْلَحَ الْمُؤْمِنُونَ

"Surely the believers are already successful."[223]

We Praise The Most High for making Us successful in this most worthy of endeavors.

Amin

---

[222] *"When is Orun?"& "Why is Orun?" of The Sunrise in the West*

[223] *Surah Muminun 23:1*

*** אַרְיֵה 224 יְהוּדָה ***
Lioness of Judah

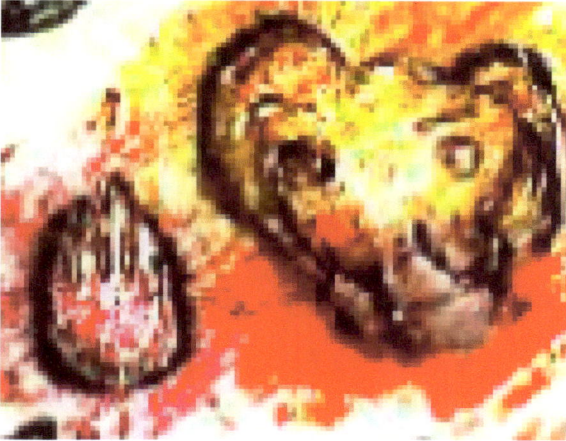

---

a.) גּוּר יְהוּדָה אַרְיֵה ר

"…*Gur Ariyah Yehudah*…" Genesis 49:9 &10

"…Judah is the Lioness' Cub[s] from the prey, my son, thou art gone up:he stooped down, he couched as a lion,

and as an old lion; who shall rouse him up?

10 The sceptre shall not depart from Judah,

nor a lawgiver from between his feet, until Shiloh come;

and unto him shall the gathering of the people be.

b.) "…Chief Lioness Goddess Priestess Princess Mary Fatimah…' -*Deipara*, page 31,

c.)on a lighter note, the Arab saying:

إذا رايـت نيوب الليـث بارزة فلا تظنــن ان
الليـث يبتسـم

When the lion bears its teeth; don't think it's smiling at you;
 rings true.

"I can't forget my history is Her Story.."-Beyonce, "Black Parade", 2020

128

U.S. : 2017
"...In that day the LORD of Hosts will become a beautiful crown
And a glorious diadem
to the remnant of His people..."[225]

Isaiah 28:5 ***Black Athena's 70th : U.S. : 6/12/2017***
₂₂₅ ***7Oaks***Revelation 12 :1-5 Authorized King James Version
^ !!! 7 !!! ^12 *And there appeared a great wonder in heaven; a woman clothedwith*the Sun, and the Moon under her feet, and upon her head a crown of twelve Stars: 2 and she being with child cried, travailing in birth, and pained to be delivered. 3 And there appeared another wonder in heaven; and behold a great red dragon, having seven heads and ten horns, and seven crowns upon his heads. 4 And his tail drew the third part of the stars of heaven, and did cast them to the earth: and the dragon stood before the woman which was ready to be delivered, for to devour her child as soon as it was born. 5 And she brought forth a man child, who was to rule all nations with a rod of iron: and her child was caught up unto God, and to his throne.*

129

نُورٌ عَلٰى نُورٍ : *Light UpOn Light*[226]

---

[226] **a.)** Surah Al Nur 24:35

بِسْمِ اللهِ الرَّحْمٰنِ الرَّحِيمِ

اللهُ نُوْرُ السَّمٰوٰتِ وَالْاَرْضِ ۚ مَثَلُ نُوْرِهٖ كَمِشْكٰوةٍ فِيْهَا
مِصْبَاحٌ ۚ الْمِصْبَاحُ فِىْ زُجَاجَةٍ ۗ الزُّجَاجَةُ كَاَنَّهَا
كَوْكَبٌ دُرِّيٌّ يُّوْقَدُ مِنْ شَجَرَةٍ مُّبٰرَكَةٍ زَيْتُوْنَةٍ لَّا شَرْقِيَّةٍ
وَّلَا غَرْبِيَّةٍ ۙ يَّكَادُ زَيْتُهَا يُضِىْٓءُ وَلَوْ لَمْ تَمْسَسْهُ نَارٌ ۗ
نُوْرٌ عَلٰى نُوْرٍ ۗ يَهْدِى اللهُ لِنُوْرِهٖ مَنْ يَّشَاءُ ۚ وَ يَضْرِبُ
اللهُ الْاَمْثَالَ لِلنَّاسِ ۗ وَاللهُ بِكُلِّ شَيْءٍ عَلِيْمٌ

Allah is the Light of the heavens and the earth.
The parable of His Light is as if there were a niche and
within it a lamp: the lamp is enclosed in glass: the glass is
a brilliant star: lit from a blessed tree, an olive, neither of
the East nor of the West, whose oil is well-nigh luminous,
through fire scarce touched it: Light upon Light! Allah doth
guide whom He will to His Light: Allah doth set forth
parables for humanity: and Allah doth know all things.

بِسْمِ اللهِ الرَّحْمٰنِ الرَّحِيمِ

... وَالنَّجْمُ وَالشَّجَرُ يَسْجُدَانِ ...

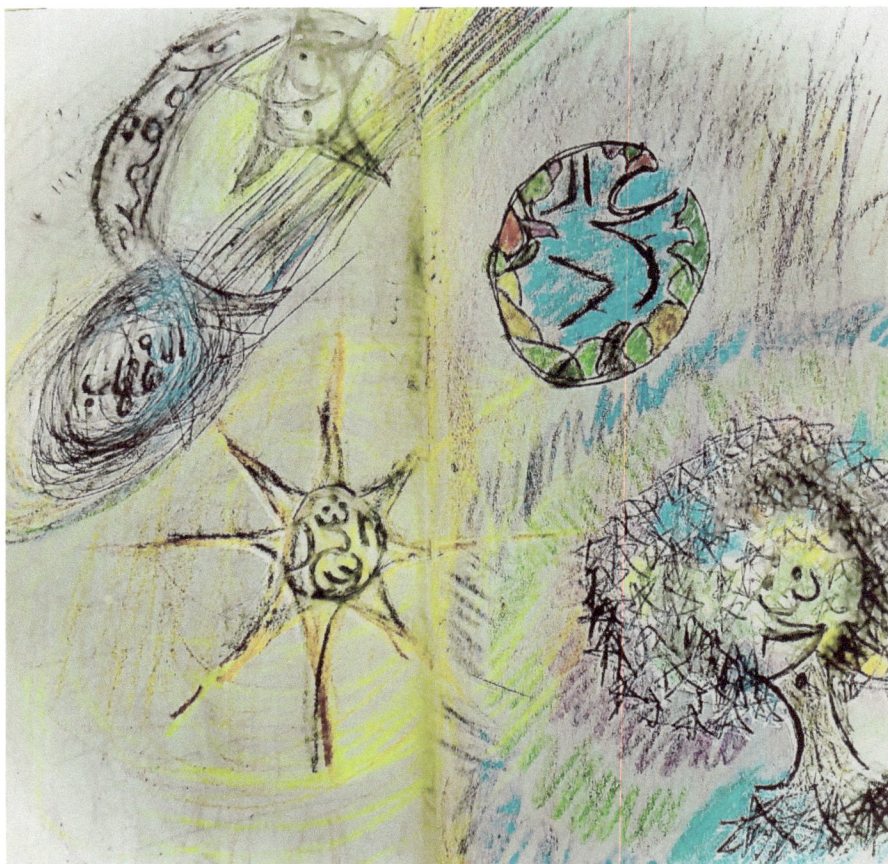

*...and the stars and the trees fall down...pen &
ink calligraphic sketch inspired by Surah Rahman
55:6 & Deuteronomy 4:19[227]

227

131

* General <u>Pike's</u> ^ <u>FreeMasonic</u> ° <u>Meteorics</u> *

Meteorics are the stuff of stars & comets, angels & demons, wishes & dreams, providence and calamity.   Meteoric descent(?) dynamizes celestial and terrestrial correspondences with mobilized verticalities that go well beyond what is called High Science.   The previously published essays, *Above & Beyond Debate : Ancient Future Mystery I & II* , relate Quranic meteoric sciences to Classical sources ; absorbing Mary Lefkowitz critiques of the historicity of   towards Freemasonry.[228]

Ancient Future Mystery understood as meteoric science, four passages have been gleaned from Albert Pike's *Morals and Dogma*[229] and shared with the reader as due diligence on the topic. Offering perspectives on initiation[230], Orun School

---

[228] Idris, Solayaan *Above & Beyond Debate : Ancient Future Mystery I & II* from the Star Logic Collection and Dusk Orientalis , Lumifont Scriptorium , 2019 & 2022

[229] Pike, Albert, Morals & Dogma of the Ancient and Accepted Scottish Rite of Freemasonry, prepared for the Supreme Council of the 33° for the Southern Jurisdiction of the United States:Charleston,1871

[230] Guénon, René. Perspectives on Initiation. United States: Sophia Perennis, 2001.

overstands the Rough Hewn and Perfect Hewn Ashlars of 1° Apprenticeship; as reference to the primitive state of humankind before and after contact with meteoric intelligence.[231] Though General Albert Pike is enshrined as the arch masonic intelligent of the United States; L'Immortal Rene Guenon cited *Morals and Dogma,*

---

[231] Pike, Albert, *Morals & Dogma of the Ancient and Accepted Scottish Rite of Freemasonry, prepared for the Supreme Council of the 33° for the Southern Jurisdiction of the United States:Charleston,1871,* 1°Apprenticeship.

as plagiarized from Eliphas Levi's *Dogme et Rituel de la Haute Magic*[232], *t*hat is *The Dogma and Ritual of High Magic*. Still *Morals and Dogma* is the seminal English language masonic ritual monitor and Pike's sparse quotations on Ancient Meteorics is shared as due diligence. We will decline to annotate General Pike's work : demarcated here, by 33°, above and below.

----

[232] a.) Lévy, Éliphas.(1854–1856). *Dogme et Rituel de la Haute Magie* [The Doctrine and Ritual of High Magic] and the English version titled, Transcendental Magic: Its Doctrine and Ritual. United Kingdom: William Rider & Son, Limited, 1923.
b.) General Albert Pike[the quintessential corporate military elite CME*]; Grand Master of the Scottish Rite for the southern jurisdiction of the United States (whose headquarters were then in Charleston), was also in touch with Blavatsky around that time. But these relations seem to have had no sequel. It would seem in this case that Pike was more clear sighted than many others, and that he quite quickly recognized with whom he was dealing. Since we have the opportunity to do so so let us add that Albert Pike's reputation as a Masonic writer was quite overrated: a considerable part of his major work Morals and Dogma of Freemasonry is clearly plaigerized from Dogme et Rituel de la Haute Magie [by the French occultist Eliphas Levi .[*Elephis Levi is most recognizable today for his rendering of the sabbatic goat, called "baphomet", used as a seal of the Church of Satan. In light of these considerations, perhaps Lefkowitz's attention would have been better turned towards Gen. Pike; rather than Dr. James*]- Guénon,René. Le Théosophisme: Histoire d'une Pseudo Religion. France: Valois, 1928.(Theosophy History of a Pseudo Religion) c.) Guenon said "…these relations *seem* to have had no sequel…" See "On Political Witchcraft: Corporate Military Elite Sorcery as Black Population Management", in this work, and "Prophetic Masonic Islam" from *The Sunrise in the West*, 2019 for further discussion.*comments in bracket are my own*

134

...Every bird which flies has the thread of the Infinite in its claw. Germination includes the hatching of a meteor, and the tap of a swallow's bill, breaking the egg; and it leads forward the birth of an earth-worm and the advent of a Socrates... — **2° - Fellow-craft**

...On each side of the temple at Paestum were fourteen, recording the Egyptian cycle of the dark and light sides of the moon, as described by Plutarch; the whole thirty-eight that surrounded them recording the two meteoric cycles so often found in the Druidic temples.
The theatre built by Scaurus, in Greece, was surrounded by 360 columns; the Temple at Mecca, and that at Iona in Scotland, by 360 stones. — **14° - GRAND ELECT, PERFECT, AND SUBLIME MASON. [Perfect Elu.}**

... Elsewhere than in Egypt, Osiris was the symbol of the refreshing rains
that descend to fertilize the earth; and Typhon the burning winds of Autumn; the stormy rains that rot the flowers, the plants, and leaves;
the short, cold days; and everything injurious in Nature, and that
produces corruption and destruction.
In short, Typhon is the principle of corruption, of darkness, of the lower world from which come earthquakes, tumultuous commotions of the air, burning heat, lightning,

and fiery meteors, and plague and pestilence. Such too was the Ahriman of the Persians; and this revolt of the Evil Principle against the Principle of Good and Light, has been represented in every cosmogony, under many varying forms. Osiris, on the contrary, by the intermediation of Isis, fills the material world with happiness, purity, and order, by which the harmony of Nature is maintained... —**25° - Knight of the Brazen Serpent (Part 1) XXV NIGHT OF THE BRAZEN SERPENT**

...What is this power of gravitation that makes everything upon the earth
tend to the centre? How does it reach out its invisible hands toward the erratic meteor-stones, arrest them in their swift course, and draw them down to the earth's bosom? It is a power. We know no more... — **26° - PRINCE OF MERCY, OR SCOTTISH TRINITARIAN.**

ooooooooooooooooooooooooooooooooooo

The appended passages from *Morals and Dogma* correlate with *StarLogic : Ancient Future Mystery I & II* and Professor Maurice Hine's "Islam and the Ancient Mysteries"; published in this work. In addition to charges of plainerism, Pike is also credited with writing the *Kloran*[233] (the ritual monitor of the KKK) . As (re)iterated in *Prophetic Masonic Islam I & II*, one need not navigate

---

[233] Kloran, Knights of the Ku Klux Klan. United States: Ku Klux Press, 1916.

by the stars while the Sun is out. Mildly, as Islamic Meteorics, Orun finds much contemporary astrology discussion to be passé. High Science pales in comparison to the Qur'an. Qur'anic commentary on civilizational meteoric development is more than necessary and sufficient. [234]

Orun in not luciferian, satanic, or diabolic, or star worshipers. Avoiding mischaracterization and following the advice to *Let not your good be evil spoken of*.[235] Abrahamic Meteorics. separates stars of Surah Rahman's[236]"fall" as in "prostrate", denoting willing submission, versus the (*rajeem*) casting down and (r)ejection of the devils, liturgically expelled , in ritual prayer and Qur'anic

---

[234] Idris, Solayaan *Above & Beyond Debate : Ancient Future Mystery I & II* from the Star Logic Collection and Dusk Orientalis , Lumifont Scriptorium , 2019 & 2022

[235] Romans 14:16 & 19 KJV *16 Let not then your good be evil spoken of:...19 Let us therefore follow after the things which make for peace, and things wherewith one may edify another..*

[236] *Surah Rahman 55:6*

بِسْـــمِ اللهِ الرَّحْمَنِ الرَّحِيمِ

... وَالنَّجْمُ وَالشَّجَرُ يَسْجُدَانِ ...

"...and the stars and the trees fall down"

recitation, referenced Surahs Mulk & Hijr[237]. Relationships between *Raheem* & *rajeem;* sublime and infernal possibilities, is   Spiritual Mystery &

---

[237] **a.)**   Surah Al Mulk

بسم اللهِ الرَّحمَنِ الرَّحيمِ

وَلَقَدْ زَيَّنَّا ٱلسَّمَاءَ ٱلدُّنْيَا بِمَصَبِيحَ وَجَعَلْنَٰهَا رُجُومًا لِّلشَّيَٰطِينِ ۖ وَأَعْتَدْنَا لَهُمْ عَذَابَٱلسَّعِيرِ

We have adorned the lowest heaven with lamps and We have made them [these lamps] a means of bombardment on the devils. (67:05)

b.)   Surah Al Hijr

بسم الله الرَّحمَنِ الرحيمِ

(6) وَأَنَّهُ كَانَ رِجَالٌ مِّنَ الْإِنسِ يَعُوذُونَ بِرِجَالٍ مِّنَ الْجِنِّ فَزَادُوهُمْ رَهَقًا(7) وَأَنَّهُمْ ظَنُّوا كَمَا ظَنَنتُمْ أَن لَّن يَبْعَثَ اللَّهُ أَحَدًا(8) وَأَنَّا لَمَسْنَا السَّمَاءَ فَوَجَدْنَاهَا مُلِئَتْ حَرَسًا شَدِيدًا وَشُهُبًا(9) وَأَنَّا كُنَّا نَقْعُدُ مِنْهَامَقَاعِدَ لِلسَّمْعِ فَمَن يَسْتَمِعِ الْآنَ يَجِدْ لَهُ شِهَابًا رَّصَدَ

(6) 'And they (came to) think as ye thought, that Allah would not raise up any one (to Judgment). (7) 'And we pried into the secrets of heaven; but we found it filled with stern guards and flaming fires. (8) 'We used, indeed, to sit there in (hidden) stations, to (steal) a hearing; but any who listen now will find a flaming fire watching him in ambush. (9) 'And we understand not whether ill is intended to those on earth, or whether their Lord (really) intends to guide them to right conduct.

c.) *Surah Al Jinn*

بسم الله الرَّحمَنِ الرحيمِ

وَلَقَدْ جَعَلْنَا فِي السَّمَاءِ بُرُوجًا وَزَيَّنَّاهَا لِلنَّاظِرِينَ (15) وَحَفِظْنَاهَا مِن كُلِّ شَيْطَانٍ رَّجِيمٍ(17) إِلَّا مَنِ اسْتَرَقَ (16) السَّمْعَ فَأَتْبَعَهُ شِهَابٌ مُبِينٌ

It is We Who have set out the zodiacal signs in the heavens, and made them fair-seeming to (all) beholders; (16) And (moreover) We have guarded them from every cursed devil: (17) But any that gains a hearing by stealth, is pursued by a flaming fire, bright (to see).fire, bright (to see).

d.) *The cherubim's "flaming sword" of Genesis 3:24 guarding the Garden of Eden is understood as a meteorite in light of these Qur'anic commentaries.*

e.) "...flaming swords; guarding Eden Torching Sodom..."- "Aerolith", Star Logic Collection, Lumifont Scriptorium, 2020

Ethical[238]Secret.   Imam Ali said, "For the true believer, paradise & hellfire present themselves at every moment."[239] *Morals and Dogma's* derivation calls one to plumb depths of the ritual work's *diabolique* source material.[240] We thus decline further analysis of General Pike's work at this time.

****

*)

We seek refuge with Allah
from knowledge that does not benefit,
from a heart that is not humbly submissive;
from a soul that is never satisfied,
and from a supplication that is not given a response.[241]

Amin

---

[238] Kashani, Fayḍ., Muhsin, Mulla., Fayḍ al-Kāshī, Muḥammad ibn Murtaḍá. Spiritual Mysteries and Ethical Secrets. United Kingdom: ICAS Press, 2012.

[239] a.) ʿAlī Ibn Abī Ṭālib., Nahjul Balagha [Peak of Eloquence]: Sermons, Letters, and Sayings of Hazrath Ali. Pakistan: Khorasan Islamic Centre, 1977.

[240] Lévy, Éliphas.(1854–1856). *Dogme et Rituel de la Haute Magie* [The Doctrine and Ritual of High Magic] and the English version titled, Transcendental Magic: Its Doctrine and Ritual. United Kingdom: William Rider & Son, Limited, 1923.

[241]

اللّهُمَّ إنّي أعوذُ بك
من علم لا ينفع
ومن قلب لا يخشع
و من نفس لا تشبع
و من دعاء لا يسمع

I shot to the top just like I'm a rocket

I ain't have a dollar inside of my pocket

Put that on my gang, I swear I ain't stoppin'

Strapped up and I'm vest up, I'm an astronaut kid

They say pain like meteorites

I got the world in my eyes

The chosen one, I got the prize

I got my niggas on my side...

—

Astronaut Kid,
YoungBoy Never Broke Again
"Until Death Call My Name Reloaded"

The Seal of Orun

Meteor Calendar 2019 - 2021[242]

Table 5. Working List of Visual Meteor Showers. Details in this Table were correct according to the best information available in June 2019, with maximum dates accurate only for 2020. The parenthesized maximum date for the Puppids-Velids indicates a reference date for the radiant only, not necessarily a true maximum. Some showers have ZHRs that vary from year to year. The most recent reliable figure is given here, except for possibly periodic showers which are noted as 'Var' = variable. For more information check the updates published e.g. in the IMO Journal WGN.

Shower	Activity	Maximum		Radiant		V_∞	r	ZHR
		Date	$\lambda_\odot$	α	δ	km/s		
Antihelion Source (ANT)	Dec 10–Sep 10	March–April, late May, late June		see Table 6		30	3.0	4
Quadrantids (010 QUA)	Dec 28–Jan 12	Jan 04	283°15	230°	+49°	41	2.1	110
γ-Ursae Minorids (404 GUM)	Jan 10–Jan 22	Jan 19	298°	228°	+67°	31	3.0	3
α-Centaurids (102 ACE)	Jan 31–Feb 20	Feb 08	319°2	210°	−59°	58	2.0	6
γ-Normids (118 GNO)	Feb 25–Mar 28	Mar 14	354°	239°	−50°	56	2.4	6
Lyrids (006 LYR)	Apr 14–Apr 30	Apr 22	32°32	271°	+34°	49	2.1	18
π-Puppids (137 PPU)	Apr 15–Apr 28	Apr 23	33°5	110°	−45°	18	2.0	Var
η-Aquariids (031 ETA)	Apr 19–May 28	May 05	45°5	338°	−01°	66	2.4	50
η-Lyrids (145 ELY)	May 03–May 14	May 08	48°0	287°	+44°	43	3.0	3
Dayt. Arietids (171 ARI)	May 14–Jun 24	Jun 07	76°6	44°	+24°	38	2.8	30
June Bootids (170 JBO)	Jun 22–Jul 02	Jun 27	95°7	224°	+48°	18	2.2	Var
Piscis Austr. (183 PAU)	Jul 15–Aug 10	Jul 27	125°	341°	−30°	35	3.2	5
S. δ-Aquariids (005 SDA)	Jul 12–Aug 23	Jul 29	127°	340°	−16°	41	2.5	25
α-Capricornids (001 CAP)	Jul 03–Aug 15	Jul 29	127°	307°	−10°	23	2.5	5
Perseids (007 PER)	Jul 17–Aug 24	Aug 12	140°0	48°	+58°	59	2.2	100
κ-Cygnids (012 KCG)	Aug 03–Aug 25	Aug 17	145°	286°	+59°	25	3.0	3
Aurigids (206 AUR)	Aug 28–Sep 05	Aug 31	158°6	91°	+39°	66	2.5	6
Sep. ε-Perseids (208 SPE)	Sep 05–Sep 21	Sep 09	166°7	48°	+40°	64	3.0	5
Dayt. Sextantids (221 DSX)	Sep 09–Oct 09	Sep 27	184°3	152°	+00°	32	2.5	5
Oct. Camelopard. (281 OCT)	Oct 05–Oct 06	Oct 05	192°58	164°	+79°	47	2.5	5
Draconids (009 DRA)	Oct 06–Oct 10	Oct 08	195°4	262°	+54°	20	2.6	10
S. Taurids (002 STA)	Sep 10–Nov 20	Oct 10	197°	32°	+09°	27	2.3	5
δ-Aurigids (224 DAU)	Oct 10–Oct 18	Oct 11	198°	84°	+44°	64	3.0	2
ε-Geminids (023 EGE)	Oct 14–Oct 27	Oct 18	205°	102°	+27°	70	3.0	3
Orionids (008 ORI)	Oct 02–Nov 07	Oct 21	208°	95°	+16°	66	2.5	20
Leonis Minorids (022 LMI)	Oct 19–Oct 27	Oct 24	211°	162°	+37°	62	3.0	2
N. Taurids (017 NTA)	Oct 20–Dec 10	Nov 12	230°	58°	+22°	29	2.3	5
Leonids (013 LEO)	Nov 06–Nov 30	Nov 17	235°27	152°	+22°	71	2.5	15
α-Monocerotids (246 AMO)	Nov 15–Nov 25	Nov 21	239°32	117°	+01°	65	2.4	Var
Nov. Orionids (250 NOO)	Nov 13–Dec 06	Nov 28	246°	91°	+16°	44	3.0	3
Phoenicids (254 PHO)	Nov 28–Dec 09	Dec 02	250°0	18°	−53°	18	2.8	Var
Puppid-Velids (301 PUP)	Dec 01–Dec 15	(Dec 07)	(255°)	123°	−45°	40	2.9	10
Monocerotids (019 MON)	Dec 05–Dec 20	Dec 09	257°	100°	+08°	41	3.0	3
σ-Hydrids (016 HYD)	Dec 03–Dec 20	Dec 09	257°	125°	+02°	58	3.0	7
Geminids (004 GEM)	Dec 04–Dec 20	Dec 14	262°2	112°	+33°	35	2.6	150
Comae Berenic. (020 COM)	Dec 12–Dec 23	Dec 16	264°	175°	+18°	65	3.0	3
Dec. L. Minorids (032 DLM)	Dec 05–Feb 04	Dec 19	268°	161°	+30°	64	3.0	5
Ursids (015 URS)	Dec 17–Dec 26	Dec 22	270°7	217°	+76°	33	3.0	10

Table 6 (next page). **Radiant positions during the year in α and δ.**

[242] From the International Meteor Society, 2019-2021

Table 5. Working List of Visual Meteor Showers. Details in this Table were corre according to the best information available in June 2020, with maximum dates accurate on for 2021. The parenthesized maximum date for the Puppids-Velids indicates a reference da for the radiant only, not necessarily a true maximum. Some showers have ZHRs that vary fro year to year. The most recent reliable figure is given here, except for possibly periodic showe which are noted as 'Var' = variable. For more information check the updates published e.g. the IMO Journal WGN.

Shower	Activity	Maximum		Radiant		V_∞	r	ZHI
		Date	$\lambda_\odot$	α	δ	km/s		
Antihelion Source (ANT)	Dec 10–Sep 10	March–April, late May, late June		see Table 6		30	3.0	4
Quadrantids (010 QUA)	Dec 28–Jan 12	Jan 03	283°15	230°	+49°	41	2.1	110
γ-Ursae Minorids (404 GUM)	Jan 10–Jan 22	Jan 19	298°	228°	+67°	31	3.0	3
α-Centaurids (102 ACE)	Jan 31–Feb 20	Feb 08	319°2	210°	−59°	58	2.0	6
γ-Normids (118 GNO)	Feb 25–Mar 28	Mar 14	354°	239°	−50°	56	2.4	6
Lyrids (006 LYR)	Apr 14–Apr 30	Apr 22	32°32	271°	+34°	49	2.1	18
π-Puppids (137 PPU)	Apr 15–Apr 28	Apr 23	33°5	110°	−45°	18	2.0	Var
η-Aquariids (031 ETA)	Apr 19–May 28	May 05	45°5	338°	−01°	66	2.4	50
η-Lyrids (145 ELY)	May 03–May 14	May 08	48°0	287°	+44°	43	3.0	3
Dayt. Arietids (171 ARI)	May 14–Jun 24	Jun 07	76°6	44°	+24°	38	2.8	30
June Bootids (170 JBO)	Jun 22–Jul 02	Jun 27	95°7	224°	+48°	18	2.2	Var
Piscis Austr. (183 PAU)	Jul 15–Aug 10	Jul 29	125°	341°	−30°	35	3.2	5
S. δ-Aquariids (005 SDA)	Jul 12–Aug 23	Jul 30	127°	340°	−16°	41	2.5	25
α-Capricornids (001 CAP)	Jul 03–Aug 15	Jul 30	127°	307°	−10°	23	2.5	5
Perseids (007 PER)	Jul 17–Aug 24	Aug 12	140°0	48°	+58°	59	2.2	100
κ-Cygnids (012 KCG)	Aug 03–Aug 25	Aug 17	145°	286°	+59°	25	3.0	3
Aurigids (206 AUR)	Aug 28–Sep 05	Sep 01	158°6	91°	+39°	66	2.5	6
Sep. ε-Perseids (208 SPE)	Sep 05–Sep 21	Sep 09	166°7	48°	+40°	64	3.0	5
Dayt. Sextantids (221 DSX)	Sep 09–Oct 09	Sep 27	184°3	152°	+00°	32	2.5	5
Oct. Camelopard. (281 OCT)	Oct 05–Oct 06	Oct 05	192°58	164°	+79°	47	2.5	5
Draconids (009 DRA)	Oct 06–Oct 10	Oct 08	195°4	262°	+54°	20	2.6	10
S. Taurids (002 STA)	Sep 10–Nov 20	Oct 10	197°	32°	+09°	27	2.3	5
δ-Aurigids (224 DAU)	Oct 10–Oct 18	Oct 11	198°	84°	+44°	64	3.0	2
ε-Geminids (023 EGE)	Oct 14–Oct 27	Oct 18	205°	102°	+27°	70	3.0	3
Orionids (008 ORI)	Oct 02–Nov 07	Oct 21	208°	95°	+16°	66	2.5	20
Leonis Minorids (022 LMI)	Oct 19–Oct 27	Oct 24	211°	162°	+37°	62	3.0	2
N. Taurids (017 NTA)	Oct 20–Dec 10	Nov 12	230°	58°	+22°	29	2.3	5
Leonids (013 LEO)	Nov 06–Nov 30	Nov 17	235°27	152°	+22°	71	2.5	10
α-Monocerotids (246 AMO)	Nov 15–Nov 25	Nov 21	239°32	117°	+01°	65	2.4	Var
Nov. Orionids (250 NOO)	Nov 13–Dec 06	Nov 28	246°	91°	+16°	44	3.0	3
Phoenicids (254 PHO)	Nov 28–Dec 09	Dec 02	250°0	18°	−53°	18	2.8	Var
Puppid-Velids (301 PUP)	Dec 01–Dec 15	(Dec 07)	(255°)	123°	−45°	40	2.9	10
Monocerotids (019 MON)	Dec 05–Dec 20	Dec 09	257°	100°	+08°	41	3.0	3
σ-Hydrids (016 HYD)	Dec 03–Dec 20	Dec 09	257°	125°	+02°	58	3.0	7
Geminids (004 GEM)	Dec 04–Dec 20	Dec 14	262°2	112°	+33°	35	2.6	150
Comae Berenic. (020 COM)	Dec 12–Dec 23	Dec 16	264°	175°	+18°	65	3.0	3
Dec. L. Minorids (032 DLM)	Dec 05–Feb 04	Dec 19	268°	161°	+30°	64	3.0	5
Ursids (015 URS)	Dec 17–Dec 26	Dec 22	270°7	217°	+76°	33	3.0	10

Table 6 (next page). **Radiant positions during the year in α and δ.**

Table 5. Working List of Visual Meteor Showers. Details in this Table were correct according to the best information available in June 2020, with maximum dates accurate only for 2021. The parenthesized maximum date for the Puppids-Velids indicates a reference date for the radiant only, not necessarily a true maximum. Some showers have ZHRs that vary from year to year. The most recent reliable figure is given here, except for possibly periodic showers which are noted as 'Var' = variable. For more information check the updates published e.g. in the IMO Journal WGN.

Shower	Activity	Maximum Date	$\lambda_\odot$	Radiant α	δ	V_∞ km/s	r	ZHR
Antihelion Source (ANT)	Dec 10–Sep 10	March–April, late May, late June	—	see Table 6		30	3.0	4
Quadrantids (010 QUA)	Dec 28–Jan 12	Jan 03	283°15	230°	+49°	41	2.1	110
γ-Ursae Minorids (404 GUM)	Jan 10–Jan 22	Jan 19	298°	228°	+67°	31	3.0	3
α-Centaurids (102 ACE)	Jan 31–Feb 20	Feb 08	319°2	210°	−59°	58	2.0	6
γ-Normids (118 GNO)	Feb 25–Mar 28	Mar 14	354°	239°	−50°	56	2.4	6
Lyrids (006 LYR)	Apr 14–Apr 30	Apr 22	32°32	271°	+34°	49	2.1	18
π-Puppids (137 PPU)	Apr 15–Apr 28	Apr 23	33°5	110°	−45°	18	2.0	Var
η-Aquariids (031 ETA)	Apr 19–May 28	May 05	45°5	338°	−01°	66	2.4	50
η-Lyrids (145 ELY)	May 03–May 14	May 08	48°0	287°	+44°	43	3.0	3
Dayt. Arietids (171 ARI)	May 14–Jun 24	Jun 07	76°6	44°	+24°	38	2.8	30
June Bootids (170 JBO)	Jun 22–Jul 02	Jun 27	95°7	224°	+48°	18	2.2	Var
Piscis Austr. (183 PAU)	Jul 15–Aug 10	Jul 29	125°	341°	−30°	35	3.2	5
S. δ-Aquariids (005 SDA)	Jul 12–Aug 23	Jul 30	127°	340°	−16°	41	2.5	25
α-Capricornids (001 CAP)	Jul 03–Aug 15	Jul 30	127°	307°	−10°	23	2.5	5
Perseids (007 PER)	Jul 17–Aug 24	Aug 12	140°0	48°	+58°	59	2.2	100
κ-Cygnids (012 KCG)	Aug 03–Aug 25	Aug 17	145°	286°	+59°	25	3.0	3
Aurigids (206 AUR)	Aug 28–Sep 05	Sep 01	158°6	91°	+39°	66	2.5	6
Sep. ε-Perseids (208 SPE)	Sep 05–Sep 21	Sep 09	166°7	48°	+40°	64	3.0	5
Dayt. Sextantids (221 DSX)	Sep 09–Oct 09	Sep 27	184°3	152°	+00°	32	2.5	5
Oct. Cameloperd. (281 OCT)	Oct 05–Oct 06	Oct 05	192°58	164°	+79°	47	2.5	5
Draconids (009 DRA)	Oct 06–Oct 10	Oct 08	195°4	262°	+54°	20	2.6	10
S. Taurids (002 STA)	Sep 10–Nov 20	Oct 10	197°	32°	+09°	27	2.3	5
δ-Aurigids (224 DAU)	Oct 10–Oct 18	Oct 11	198°	84°	+44°	64	3.0	2
ε-Geminids (023 EGE)	Oct 14–Oct 27	Oct 18	205°	102°	+27°	70	3.0	3
Orionids (006 ORI)	Oct 02–Nov 07	Oct 21	208°	95°	+16°	66	2.5	20
Leonis Minorids (022 LMI)	Oct 19–Oct 27	Oct 24	211°	162°	+37°	62	3.0	2
N. Taurids (017 NTA)	Oct 20–Dec 10	Nov 12	230°	58°	+22°	29	2.3	5
Leonids (013 LEO)	Nov 06–Nov 30	Nov 17	235°27	152°	+22°	71	2.5	10
α-Monocerotids (246 AMO)	Nov 15–Nov 25	Nov 21	239°32	117°	+01°	65	2.4	Var
Nov. Orionids (250 NOO)	Nov 13–Dec 06	Nov 28	246°	91°	+16°	44	3.0	3
Phoenicids (254 PHO)	Nov 28–Dec 09	Dec 02	250°0	18°	−53°	18	2.8	Var
Puppid-Velids (301 PUP)	Dec 01–Dec 15	(Dec 07)	(255°)	123°	−45°	40	2.9	10
Monocerotids (019 MON)	Dec 05–Dec 20	Dec 09	257°	100°	+08°	41	3.0	3
σ-Hydrids (016 HYD)	Dec 03–Dec 20	Dec 09	257°	125°	+02°	58	3.0	7
Geminids (004 GEM)	Dec 04–Dec 20	Dec 14	262°2	112°	+33°	35	2.6	150
Comae Beranic. (020 COM)	Dec 12–Dec 23	Dec 16	264°	175°	+18°	65	3.0	3
Dec. L. Minorids (032 DLM)	Dec 05–Feb 04	Dec 19	268°	161°	+30°	64	3.0	5
Ursids (015 URS)	Dec 17–Dec 26	Dec 22	270°7	217°	+76°	33	3.0	10

Table 6 (next page). **Radiant positions during the year in** α **and** δ.

144

""Be" and it is", 2

A

African Union, 20,52,54
Afro Arabic, 1,38,92,95,116
Afrocentrism,60,88,89,94,96,111
A g e (s), 25,79,91,102105,112-16
Alma Mater, 33
Alexander, 80,93
American Descendants of Slavery(ADOS), 2,13,14,43,44,47,49,53,70,72,73,90,103,107,114,121
a n c e s t o r s, 14,23,30,90,115
A n c i e n t Mystery,75-79,81-83,87,92,94,108,111,112,119-122
Andalusia, 12, 56, 92,100
Angelic, 104- 106,110-11
A r a b i c, 1,2,12,14,38,56,75,79,90,91,92,99,100,102,105,113,116
Aristotle,80,91,95

B

b e l i e v e r s, 8,18,30,64,84,122
Bernal, Martin/ *Black Athena*,88,89,92,94,95,100,117
Black August, 22,28,37,39,40,42,43,45,46
Black Muslims, 51,98
Birds, 16-18,114
Bronze Age, 114
Browder Files, 36,40

145

147

148

www.ingramcontent.com/pod-product-compliance
Lightning Source LLC
Chambersburg PA
CBHW041917260326
41914CB00013B/1477